SLASH

SLASH

EXCESS: THE DEFINITIVE BIOGRAPHY

PAUL STENNING

MUSIC PRESS

Published by Music Press Books
an imprint of John Blake Publishing Ltd,
3 Bramber Court, 2 Bramber Road,
London W14 9PB, England

www.johnblakebooks.com

www.facebook.com/johnblakebooks
twitter.com/jblakebooks

Previously published by Independent Music Press as *Slash – Surviving Guns N' Roses, Velvet Revolver & Rock's Snake Pit* in 2006
This edition published in 2017

ISBN: 978 1 78606 419 6

All rights reserved. No part of this publication may be reproduced, stored in a retrieval system, or transmitted in any form or by any means, without the prior permission in writing of the publisher, nor be otherwise circulated in any form of binding or cover other than that in which it is published and without a similar condition including this condition being imposed on the subsequent purchaser.

British Library Cataloguing-in-Publication Data:

A catalogue record for this book is available from the British Library.

Design by www.envydesign.co.uk

Printed in Great Britain by CPI Group (UK) Ltd

1 3 5 7 9 10 8 6 4 2

© Text copyright Paul Stenning 2017

The right of Paul Stenning to be identified as the author of this work has been asserted by him in accordance with the Copyright, Designs and Patents Act 1988.

Papers used by John Blake Publishing are natural, recyclable products made from wood grown in sustainable forests. The manufacturing processes conform to the environmental regulations of the country of origin.

Every attempt has been made to contact the relevant copyright-holders, but some were unobtainable. We would be grateful if the appropriate people could contact us.

John Blake Publishing is an imprint of Bonnier Publishing
www.bonnierpublishing.com

CONTENTS

ACKNOWLEDGEMENTS

Many thanks to Steven Adler, Vicky Hamilton, Perla Hudson, Ruben MacBlue, Johnny Kreis, Jordan Tyler, Shari Black Velvet, Keri Kelli, Jus Kaber, Stefanos Metal Eagle, Lakis Kyraciou, and all the people who contributed or helped in some way.

Tommy Vance R.I.P. 1941–2005.

Dedicated to my wonderful wife, Isla.

INTRODUCTION

Is there a bigger icon in the world of rock music than Slash? With his frizzy hair obscuring his face, top hat perched on his crown, cigarette permanently dangling from his mouth and bottle of Jack Daniels by his side, there are few people in the world who would not recognise him.

It's due to this indelible image that Slash has graced thousands of music magazine covers and been interviewed by every type of publication under the sun. Slash is not just a brilliant guitarist, he is an icon and a marker of rock 'n' roll excess and cool. He has experienced pretty much everything one associates with the nefarious world of rock and, unlike many of his peers, he has lived to tell the tale with continuing humility and good grace.

His generation of rockers has its share of drooling, junkie fuck ups, but somehow Slash has managed to retain his cool charm throughout drug and alcohol use that would have wrecked lesser individuals. Indeed, he has commented that people often say he looks younger than his forty-plus years and that they expect him to look more "addled".

Quite how he has emerged so scar-free from numerous excessive years is unclear but this is a character who permanently stands on the precipice of decadence yet somehow keeps his head clear and his guitar playing immaculate. Though he is now a global symbol of rock 'n' roll – for sheer distinctive image alone – he made his name with an ability to ring an impressive succession of notes from his permanent axe companion, a sunburst Gibson Les Paul. Slash can play rhythm guitar with a composed insouciance and he shreds solos like you or I pour milk.

Such legends are not made, they are born. Considering his rock 'n' roll upbringing, Slash was perhaps destined to become a star himself and the writing was on the wall early in his career. As a very young man, he played guitar on one of the best selling albums of all-time, Guns N' Roses' *Appetite For Destruction*. It was the success of this record that propelled two of its members to global stardom. Frontman Axl Rose was an instant icon but Slash too achieved the kind of success that results from being one half of a truly enigmatic partnership. Not since Jagger and Richards or Page and Plant had such a riotous combination of vocal wonder and guitar genius been established. This rare duality made Axl and Slash superstars although they both accepted the honour with notably different approaches.

Axl thrived on the limelight whilst Slash shunned it, hiding behind his mop of curly hair. Axl swaggered and floated across the stage, while Slash threw his head in a tangle of head-banging glory, for all the world looking as if he were some kid pretending to be a rock star in front of his bedroom mirror. Except he was the real deal. In numerous interviews, the Guns N' Roses singer frequently caused controversy, becoming known as a fiery superstar; Slash, meanwhile, was always available with a laugh and a smile. Keep him stocked in Jack & Coke and he was devotedly yours.

Like all the best and most successful rock partnerships, it was this paradox of behaviour which served the double act so well. They were chalk and cheese, Axl said tom-Ah-to, Slash baulked, tom-A-to. Yet out of this clash of styles, some of the greatest rock music of all time emerged and many people felt, with the greatest of respect to the other members, that G N' R was predominantly about Axl and Slash. In their unavoidable clashes, the two prompted certain fans to favour one over the other. The volatile frontman wannabes preferred Axl while the low slung six-string pretenders picked Slash. Whatever your preference, everyone sensed the band would not truly work without one or the other.

With inner turmoil and inevitable arguments over musical style and money, the original incarnation of Guns N' Roses was destined to disintegrate – their collective career as the ultimate five-piece was short. Slash stayed longer than his guitar partner Izzy Stradlin, he outlasted childhood friend Steven Adler and avoided the inevitable split from Axl as long as he could. Yet the writing was on the wall and after a decade of ties, Slash moved on.

Without Slash, can Guns N' Roses ever possibly be the same? For some, it is debatable that the guitarist was equally as important to their success and proficiency as Axl Rose. He was the one who still managed to wake early, handle interviews without complaint, and he who would always make a show on time and on form.

The late 1990s were less than eventful for the top-hatted one, but he somehow remained in the minds of numerous rockers around the world, initially with apparent side project Slash's Snakepit. Yet, it was not until he created a super-group, with the help of ex-G N' R bassist Duff McKagan and drummer Matt Sorum and a consummate frontman in ex-Stone Temple Pilots throat Scott Weiland, that Slash once again enjoyed the glare of world attention. With Velvet Revolver, he returned to his glory days with G N' R, all the while smoking Marlboro and slugging Old No. 7.

Contrary to some cynical suggestions, Velvet Revolver are anything but a one hit wonder. Despite previous drug problems and subsequent jail time for Weiland, the band seem able to stick to their touring commitments and keep the VR name in the spotlight. With a carefree attitude and typically brazen playing, Slash has become the focal point of the band and continues to release top quality recordings featuring his guitar efforts; meanwhile, Axl Rose sits on a ticking time bomb in the shape of his *Chinese Democracy* album which, at the time of writing, has taken a whopping fourteen years and counting to make.

SLASH

Given Slash is such an enduring icon, it is a surprise there has not previously been a biography written on his life, and his part in the rock 'n' roll massacre of G N' R and beyond. With this in mind, this book hopes to uncover information on his tale and how he became one of the greatest guitar players of the modern music era. By examining his role in all the key albums of his career and by investigating his personal life, we will see how a polite, understated English kid traversed the international music community and became a hero for aspiring guitarists and rock 'n' roll down 'n' outs the world over. This is Slash's untamed story and a homage to his abilities and attitude.

Long may he reign as the six-string King.

* * *

Slash is famously quiet, shy and hard to figure out. However, in tracing his history, it is possible to find the man behind the veil. The story of Guns N' Roses has been told many times before, but it is a tale that is vital to understand how Slash came to be where he is and who he is. If you already know certain parts of the story then press on, because there are plenty of revelations within the G N' R saga, previously unexplored. But most importantly, this is the first book to examine the catalogue of other work by Slash, which have been regularly brushed under the carpet by so-called rock experts. How many times has someone ignored the fantastic and consistent Slash's Snakepit? If Slash had formed Velvet Revolver with an unknown singer, then his most recent band might well have suffered a similar, low profile fate to Snakepit. This is a shame because everything Slash has ever put his name to has always been quality rock music blessed with his trademark guitar style.

So there is an in-depth look into Slash's projects post-Guns N' Roses, which includes everything from his Blues Ball outfit to the ongoing super group, Velvet Revolver. Again, given Revolver's impression on the rock scene, their story is somewhat familiar. I can make no apologies for tracing the lineage of their search for a singer and their debut album *Contraband*, but there should be plenty you have never read before. Although this is a personal biography of Slash, there has to be the context of his surrounding friends and band mates in all his past musical endeavours. In examining his close associates, it is where we often learn the most about Slash himself.

So forgive this for not being the regular solo biography. It is a broader examination of a man with a phenomenal talent. For someone so famous and recognisable there is still much we don't know of Slash but that is as it should be and his mystique is part of the allure. He is markedly different in attitude and personality than his ex-cohort Axl Rose, but the one similarity they share is they don't give much away. Therefore there is nothing here that will tell you when Slash last used hairspray (if ever) or where he bought his first top hat, but there *is* an extensive section of interesting facts I have uncovered. The 'Did You Know?' chapter is easy to delve into and will give you some quick, lesser known snippets. Elsewhere, this is a full examination of the music Slash has been a part of – after all, that is the most important thing. Aside from his noticeable image, this is where you can learn the most about the true Slash. Every guitar lick, every chord change and every strained backing vocal.

My first initiation into the world of Slash came when I heard a friend's copy of *Appetite For Destruction*. At the time I was in the first year of Big Boy's school. The exercise books we used were soon decorated with my drawings of the most obvious member of the band. He wore that top hat, his hair obscured his face and he looked cooler than James Dean. Yeah, Axl was the primary focus of the band, always, but Slash held your interest too. It was almost confusing how he could look so wasted yet play such incendiary guitar. How did he supposedly control his "windmill" hands enough to wring out those impeccable riffs? Anyone who has tried to learn the opening bars of 'Sweet Child O' Mine' as an aspiring guitarist realises the stuff Slash plays is harder than it looks (trust me I know).

So, from seeing a very young Slash who just looked every inch the rock 'n' roll rebel, fans soon understood he didn't get to be where he is by sheer luck, or by virtue of his identifiable look. Much like one of his heroes, AC/DC's Angus Young, Slash has a very recognisable image but it is not contrived and sometimes this takes away from his awesome ability as a guitarist.

As the years progressed Guns N' Roses became a deeper, more serious affair, for better or for worse. Slash felt uncomfortable with this overblown transition, but for G N' R fans the music took on an epic edge, the lyrics being poetic and lovelorn. Though the chief guitar player felt at odds with this poker-faced version of a rock band, he nevertheless employed greater restraint in his playing and never failed to emotionally rouse an audience.

Even Axl would concede Slash could always play

awesome guitar. That says it all about a man who has had more than his fair share of rock 'n' roll excess. There were many nights where Slash held the wayward Gunners together. Even though Axl once addressed his guitarist's drug use in front of a hundred thousand people, the mild-mannered six stringer took it on the chin and carried on playing, apparently unaffected.

Without Slash, there is no doubt Guns N' Roses could have collapsed long before they had time to produce the *Use Your Illusion* albums. Having written the history of Guns N' Roses (twice in fact), I was accused by thousands of readers of solely concentrating on Axl Rose and his contribution to the band, as if I only thought he was worthy of examination. I tell you what I told them – it was not intentional. There is no Guns N' Roses without Axl, even more so these days, but that is understating the contribution of the other members. It was not just Slash and Axl either. Slash's good friend Duff had a lot to do with the chemistry the band enjoyed and was one of the more noticeable members with his lanky stance and bleached blonde hair.

G N' R was simply one of those bands whose chemistry was a huge part of their success. That is why their immense productivity could only last so long.

INTRODUCTION

Once they hit mega stardom, many of the band, Slash included, felt alienated by such attention. This destroyed the band's unity and unique je ne sais quoi. But in my mind, it is quite simple. There would not have been the Guns N' Roses as we know it without two men. One is Axl and the other is Slash.

In another element of contrast, Axl remains a bachelor; Slash, meanwhile, has now fathered two children, has a happy marriage and by all accounts has matured a lot. Yet for fans, he is still the same ol' Slash we know and love. The more things change, the more he stays the same. Always approaching repetitive and irritating interviews with the same acceptance and respect. He doesn't play for the money, but for the thrill and the sheer joy of plugging away at his Les Paul. Oh yes, he still owns the same guitar he has played since being a teenager – how many other people do that?

So take a ride through the career of one of rock's leading figures and see how he developed from being a shy, British kid into an American superstar. It is a story like no other and, if you follow closely, I am sure you will experience a new found respect for one of the most unassuming and genuine people that the world of music has ever produced.

Chapter 1

CAN YOU HEAR THE MUSIC?

**"THE KIDS AROUND ME CHANGED,
AND SUDDENLY I GOT MORE POPULAR
BECAUSE I WAS A GUITAR PLAYER".**
SLASH

The origins of one of the world's best known guitarists could not have been more at odds with his eventual glamorous surroundings. Little Saul Hudson came into the world in a hospital in Hampstead, London on July 23, 1965. Though the borough situated in Camden in the English capital was not exactly known for its production of rock talent, it does have a prodigious history of residents: Charles Dickens, Sir Richard Burton, Agatha Christie, Florence Nightingale and George Orwell were all known to have lived there at some point during their lives; also, in keeping with the borough's creative reputation, a number of artistic, literary and intellectual institutions are stationed there. Perhaps it's not surprising therefore that Hampstead

1

commands some of the highest house prices in the United Kingdom.

1965 was a pivotal year for many reasons. Politically, the Vietnam War was slowly gaining momentum and in March, 3500 U.S. Marines moved into South Vietnam. This was the first time American troops had settled in the country and it precipitated further warring tactics, which were to build into the full scale war a few years later. Malcolm Little, better known as Malcolm X, was assassinated in New York City on February 21, 1965. The Black Muslim leader and Nation Of Islam spokesperson had turned a life of crime into a platform where he could speak out on human rights, black pride and economic self-reliance for the black race ... until he was assassinated.

In the entertainment world, 1965 was a crucial year. Slash shares his year of birth with other eventual influential and infamous musicians such as Trent Reznor (Nine Inch Nails), Krist Novoselic (Nirvana), Greg Graffin (Bad Religion) and Dexter Holland (Offspring). Surprisingly, Slash is the only Guns N' Roses member to have been born into a rock 'n' roll family. He has said he was "fortunate to have been exposed to so much over-indulgent, egotistical, just basically ridiculous rock 'n' roll environment. I watched all these things go down.

I watched people go down. I watched a lot of heavy shit go down and I learned from it."

Slash was christened Saul by his Jewish/English father Anthony and black American mother Ola, who was of Nigerian descent. Later, his full name would be abbreviated thanks to a family friend. Slash's father Anthony was a graphic design artist who created several album covers for various rock musicians (including Joni Mitchell's *Court And Spark* LP) while his mother Ola was a clothes designer. She even designed the costumes for the movie *The Man Who Fell To Earth* starring David Bowie. Slash's mother and Bowie actually began to date for two years shortly after the Hudsons divorced. But this came later.

Before this, the family inexplicably moved from the quaint area of London — where incidentally arty Slash's hangout was the Natural History Museum — to somewhere far less exotic, the West Midlands region of Stoke-On-Trent, close to northern England. Here was a town miles from anywhere of any interest — its only other musical claim to fame is the fact that both Robbie Williams (interestingly, like Williams, Slash played soccer whilst living in England) and Lemmy Kilmister of Motorhead were born there; the town also has a high class reputation for pottery.

The Hudson family remained in England until Slash was eleven. Ola sought to move back to America and took Slash with her, while Anthony remained in England, perhaps an ominous precursor to their future divorce. Slash and his mother settled in Laurel Canyon, an area in Hollywood Hills in Los Angeles, California. It was a world away from the cold, dank streets of working-class Stoke. Though Ola Hudson was an American citizen, Slash was, of course, still a Brit. But times were changing. Since the mid-1960s in fact, the immigration laws were changed to accommodate increasing numbers of visitors from other countries. In the year Slash was born, then-President Lyndon B. Johnson boldly signed a bill which would subsequently encourage people of other nationalities to move and settle in America. This proposal helped to turn America into a cosmopolitan country as suddenly national origin was not the basis for the right to house yourself in the land of the free. The 'American Dream' was now open to anyone, and it was something Slash would soon to take advantage of … not that he knew it at the time.

Initially, he was viewed with suspicion by classmates at his new school, Fairfax High. Slash was a cool little kid at home, where there were often hippy, rock 'n' roller visitors who approved of the fuzzy haired boy. Yet it must be remembered, Slash entered California with a very obvious English accent. As anyone who has come across a Stoke native knows, that particular Midlands variation of speech is very distinctive, often grating and perhaps one of the hardest accents to shake off. Eventually Slash would manage it, as a combination of being raised in Los Angeles and developing his new accent to fit in with the other kids eventually banished his dreary Stoke brogue.

The residents of Fairfax High School should have embraced Saul Hudson, for their establishment was hot on producing artistic talent. Musically the likes of Red Hot Chili Peppers duo Anthony Kiedis and Michael Balzary (better known as Flea), along with future Slash mate Lenny Kravitz, were to become famous former attendees. There were also cameos for actors Demi Moore and David Arquette. Indeed, the school developed a steady reputation of providing a breeding ground for several major entertainment figures from the 1930s to the 1980s. Many years after Slash left the hallowed halls, the school became notorious for a far less savoury reason. In January 1993 a student went to school with a gun in his possession. The piece accidentally fired, killing one student and injuring another.

Whilst at Fairfax, Slash was almost *too* cool with his long hair, jeans and t-shirts – coming across as too hippy, too laid back for the conservative area he now lived in. Luckily, while school was initially a life of boredom and exile from his peers, Slash's home life was far more agreeable. As the guitarist would later explain, his parents were still maintaining their hippy outlook and this, coupled with their respective professions, attracted numerous bohemian and colourful sorts to the Hudson household. There were regular appearances for Rolling Stones' Ronnie Wood, Joni Mitchell, David Geffen (a future professional acquaintance of Slash) and, most impressively, David Bowie and Iggy Pop.

"The reason I know Ron Wood from when I was so young is because I was raised in the music business and I've always known all the people my parents worked with in some way, shape or form," Slash would later recall on www.arocknid.com. "I met Ron Wood over at a guy named Seymour Cassel's house, which was behind the Hyatt Hollywood, and his son was my best friend in Junior High School in Los Angeles. We pretty much ditched all of school and spent most of our time at Seymour's house smoking pot, growing pot – basically the whole gang of bad kids used to hang out there. Well, not the bad kids but all the misfits or whatever. He's a tough motherfucker and he used to call me [Slash] and it just stuck. I asked him why years later and he goes, 'Because you're always in some hurry or doing a deal or hustling something' … Every time I came over to the house he'd go, 'Hey Slash!' and that's the most conversation we ever had!"

Slash later expressed his belief that being around such artistic talents, and seeing the perils of rock 'n' roll decadence first hand, helped him to maintain his cool in the face of adversity in the music business. After all, he may only have barely hit puberty, but the succession of famous musicians stirred a passion in the young boy.

"I was exposed to neurotic musicians ever since I was a little kid. I used to love the look of the equipment," he would explain on www.belowempty.com, "the concerts, getting into the venue and seeing the place filling up with people, the stage, the lights, the whole thing."

And whether he knew it or not, it also ignited that spark of rebellion, the laid-back and carefree attitude of a rock 'n' roll drifter. There were drugs and alcohol around and though this was not a pastime indulged in front of Slash, there was certainly a subliminal intake of adrenalin when Iggy Pop or David Bowie were present.

The former has long been a hi-octane, gasoline fuelled rock 'n' roll monster. There's no blood cursing through the veins of the man formerly known as James Newell Osterberg – just paraffin. But at the time Slash was first adapting to high school, Iggy Pop was checking himself into a mental institution. This was a bold attempt at trying to wean himself off class A drugs. Before the early 1980s, there were no such things as Rehab Centres, which perhaps explains how so many iconic drug addicted musicians and artists perished in the 1960s and 1970s.

Pop and Bowie were friends, to the point where Bowie was a regular visitor as Pop tried to clean up. Later, the pair would tour together, though Iggy was merely a spectator on the *Station To Station* tour as Bowie's fame increased. Still later, Bowie would also need to come clean drug wise and he moved to Berlin in order to dry out, sharing an apartment with, yes, Iggy Pop. The two would also work together, producing some awe-inspiring music. Yet with Ola Hudson eventually dating Bowie, an enigmatic and addictive personality – coupled with the visits of other creatives, Slash simply had to soak it up. The decadence, the highs, the perils and the heartache. It was in his blood from an early age and this schooling would soon prove both useful and dangerous.

By the mid-1970s, relations were strained between Mr and Mrs Hudson and they agreed it would be best for them to divorce. With all the melee in his home life, and no small amount of upset at his parents' split, Slash moved in with his grandmother, initially only temporarily. As part of his distress, Slash began a familiar pattern of behaviour. When he was pissed off or upset, rather than sit and curse his luck or sulk, he would get out there and do something constructive. As a youngster in the 1970s, one of the most productive hobbies was BMX riding. Virtually as soon as he was instilled in his grandmother's home, he discovered this passion for biking. He also made friends from the venture, riding with fellow fanatics and eventually winning several awards on the way to near-professional status.

Looking back at his subsequent success and fame, you might assume that there was some grand design to his life and career choice, but in fact nothing could be further from the truth. As Slash later admitted in *Guitar* magazine, when asked what he wanted to do with his life, "I had no fuckin' clue! I was racing bikes and … somehow I started playing guitar and that was it. I didn't have any long-term goals. When I started playing guitar I didn't even think about it as being my career. I'm a huge rock fan and would have loved to have been a big rock star but I spent most of my time learning how to play the fuckin' thing and stuff like that. Then you just sort of live day by day just trying to get better at what you're doing."

From BMX to guitar was actually not that big a leap. Both interests require a certain individuality and within both hobbies you can instil your own personality. There is no "right" way to play guitar just as there is no set standard to riding a bike, other than to stay balanced. The great thing about both is you could take the bike or the instrument where *you* wanted to go – naturally this unique streak is what appealed to Slash. Besides it was a given he would be interested in music, having spent a large part of his youth as a voyeur of the movers and shakers of the rock scene. It's ironic therefore that Slash did not actually profess an interest in learning an instrument until he was away from the bohemian environment of his parents' house. He was no child prodigy. He was not forced into learning an instrument at a ridiculously young age, rather he was left to his own devices and, once away from the hullabaloo of a rock 'n' roll habitat, he brought his own form of music to his grandmother's house.

She approved and positively encouraged Slash to nurture his interest, even providing him with his very first guitar. It seemed strange that a guitar would be lying around her garage and not his parents' but that was the case. The instrument was of the classical acoustic style, which meant the strings were nylon as opposed to steel. As anyone who has tried to play a steel-strung guitar knows, at first it can seriously hurt the tips of your fingers, at least until your skin becomes accustomed to the tough material. Playing on nylon strings is more comfortable but in this instance what made it truly easy for Slash was the fact that his first guitar only had one string.

By default the musical options were limited, but this actually helped. It is far easier to become accustomed to a guitar neck with only one string because there is little to distract you from adapting to the shape and feel of the guitar itself. When there are the requisite six strings, the immediate reaction is to try and play all at once. When you look into the basics of guitar, everything centres around chords rather than individual strings. Chords are, of course, the root of guitar playing, rhythm in particular, but there is no easier way to adapt to a guitar than practising with one string and observing how each move of fret changes the sound of the string. Therefore, with this one important string, Slash managed to learn the mammoth riff to Deep Purple's 'Smoke On The Water'. Though the song is essentially simple, the young Slash instantly mastered the impact of a strong yet simple riff, lending him good experience for his later ventures with six strings.

In tandem with a growing confidence at school, Slash increasingly fell upon the guitar as a means to express himself. As Slash was apparently a natural and seemed to enjoy tinkering around with the lumpen wood for pleasure, his grandmother further encouraged his interest and bought him his first proper electric guitar – a copy of a Gibson Explorer. "I flipped out on it," Slash later explained to *Kerrang!* "Unfortunately, it was a piece of crap. I used to fuck up around the house, and my grandmother would chase me around the couch. She'd freak out when I'd play [Led Zeppelin's] 'Black Dog' really loud." Slash's influences had been picked up through a combination of his parents' record collection and their friends' occupations. Thus Led Zeppelin, Eric Clapton,

CAN YOU HEAR THE MUSIC?

Aerosmith, Queen, Jeff Beck and AC/DC were early inspirations for Slash and his developing talent.

Every new guitar player considers taking lessons to improve and Slash was no different. Yet, with a devilish independent streak, he quickly decided that he wasn't receiving ideal tuition from his chosen teacher and proceeded to tutor himself by listening to records and finding notes on the guitar simply from some inner inspiration and a natural ear. The instrument was a godsend to the young rocker in waiting and it instantly eclipsed any academic aspirations he might have harboured. In fact, Slash gradually stopped going to school altogether, instead focusing on learning new and exciting techniques on his Gibson and rapidly developing as a player. By the eleventh grade, at age fifteen, Slash dropped out of school permanently. "I'm real single-minded, so once I got into guitar, that's all I did. It basically replaced school." At least school had provided one intriguing prospect. Though they would not collaborate until some years later, Slash counted one (future guitarist) Dave Kushner among his fellow pupils. "We got into trouble, but not, like, together. I think maybe we smoked pot once together…" Kushner recounted three decades later, "but we were just around each other a lot. We were friends, you know, but he was doing his thing and I was doing mine. I had just started playing guitar right before High School when he was already ripping.'"

It is revealing to note that where schoolmates felt Slash was highly accomplished, he was himself less convinced and, with typical humility, would eventually describe his early years of learning guitar on www.home.swipnet.se as follows. "I had no idea what I was doing, so I carried it around with me everywhere I went. I quit school and had a full-time job to support it, and I spent all my time just trying to figure out what I was doing. Anytime I heard something, I'd try to learn it. I'd learn all the bass parts and all the different voices. [So] if it was a Jeff Beck thing, I had to learn that. And if I didn't pull it off by the end of the night, I wouldn't sleep. That's typical of me with anything. I have a real addictive personality: I get into something, and I do it to the hilt."

Such devotion can cause frustration. As Slash was becoming more proficient he noticed there really was no substitute for a well-made, expensive guitar. He soon progressed to a Memphis Les Paul copy, but as he once recalled, "I ended up sticking it through a wall, neck first, because I could not keep the thing in tune!" And he retained his streak of impudence when "playing not practising" guitar. "I might learn one particular solo off one song on one record, maybe even just one section. I don't like playing scales and I hate the word 'practise'. What I do is play all the time. I'm a really neurotic guitar player."

Something Slash also noticed was how people changed their perception of him once he carried a guitar with him. With his tousled long hair and assured demeanour, a guitar was a natural companion and it was not just the boys who started to think he was cool. Now, for the first time, Slash was attracting girls and began to date them. Was it this easy he wondered? All you have to do is play guitar and look good and the chicks start to get interested? He was about to find out.

As the 1980s dawned, he was about to embark on a very special career where girls, money and fame were the norm.

Chapter 2

WE ARE THE ROAD CREW

"HE'LL BE REALLY QUIET MOST OF THE TIME AND WON'T REALLY LET A LOT OF HIMSELF OUT. THEN HE PULLS ON A GUITAR AND LET'S OUT HIS HEART AND SOUL."
AXL ROSE ON SLASH

It is a natural progression for any improving musician to seek others to rehearse and develop with. No matter how independent an artist is, as he/she develops their craft, it is instinctive to showcase their ideas to others and – in many ways – find out how good they actually are. Slash was fiercely autonomous and self-sufficient but not in a clandestine, selfish manner. He was sociable, likeable and made friends easily, even more so now he had gained a deep-rooted self-confidence from playing guitar. Slash was still young and as such, when he wasn't improving on guitar he was hanging around with other children riding bikes or sometimes skateboards. It was during an impromptu skateboard session that Slash and Steven Adler fell upon each other. Though both had attended the same school, they didn't initially realise it and, besides, their only interest was in escaping classes. So they did what any self-respecting budding muso does and formed the nucleus of their first band. Adler would sit with Slash and bang obtrusively on a guitar plugged into a small amplifier, turned up as loud as it would go.

Born six months before Slash on January 22, Steven Adler grew up in Cleveland, Ohio but moved to Los Angeles when he was still a young boy. Originally Steven wanted to be a guitarist but quickly decided he didn't have the patience for such an instrument. He then tried singing but, realising his voice was not strong enough, he opted for an instrument which had always been in the background: drums. As a very young boy he would bang on any pots and pans he could find around the house and it was this natural vocation he eventually turned into a full-time, hugely successful occupation. He began to save up for his first proper drum kit.

"I lived about five or six blocks from Santa Monica Blvd," Adler said to www.gnrsource.com, "so if I was with Slash, we'd get back to my house first, I had two rooms, a living room, and a bedroom, and I'd always sleep in the living room. In the bedroom, I had this guitar and a little amplifier that I was learning to play, and one day I just showed it to Slash. I knew two chords and two scales and I tried to play along to *Kiss Alive*, strike all the Ace Frehley positions, man! Well, Slash just fell in love with that guitar. I gave it to him, and within a week he was writing songs. He was just made for the guitar. Made for it. I just wanted to be a rock 'n' roll star, the guitar was too complicated for me. I set up all these pillows and coat hangers and got my first drumsticks and played along to Kiss and Boston. Music made me feel special. Rock 'n' roll is in my heart and in my soul and the lifestyle was a huge part of it. It's like, sex and rock 'n' roll, that was the lifestyle I was living, right from then. It was never heavy drugs at that age. I was a big pothead, that's what I liked, the three P's man – pot, pussy and percussion! We had *way* more fun before we got success than after."

With this rudimentary set-up, Slash and Steven could finally put their first version of a group together. Steven was a natural drummer, possessed with accurate timing, rhythm and balance while Slash was by now a very proficient guitarist. The two played the music of their rock heroes such as Aerosmith and the Rolling Stones.

Slash and Steven were also friends outside of playing music as Adler explained, "Me and Slash would walk up and down Sunset and Hollywood Boulevards," he told www.gnrsource.com, "and each day we had this thing where we'd take a different type of alcohol, and we'd walk up and down, and what we'd be talking about was how we'd be living when we were rock and roll stars, it was like this dream that I always knew would come true."

Soon the boys had the nucleus of a full band which they named Road Crew and though the other members were not as accomplished as Slash and Steven, the outfit did at least steer them in the direction of a bass player who was to become a long time associate. Michael 'Duff' McKagan was born in Seattle on February 5, 1965 and like Slash and Steven had upped sticks to L.A., moon-lighting in bands ever since. McKagan had played drums or bass for a throng of New Wave or Seattle punk bands including the Fastbacks, Fartz, Silly Killers, Vain and 10 Minute Warning, but left the chilly and wet Northwest for sunny south California in 1985.

In true punk, fashion he'd initially fumbled around on various instruments including guitar. His brother Bruce had taught him his first chords on a bass and Duff was to stick with this instrument after deciding that he was less likely to make an impression in the guitar capital of rock 'n' roll. The lanky blonde-haired Seattleite came from a prominent musical background – most of his eight siblings could play at least one instrument and his father had sung in a barber shop quartet. "In Seattle back in my formative years as a musician, I played drums, bass and guitar. I couldn't figure out what I wanted to play," Duff would later attest in *Metal Hammer*. "I got a record by Prince and was like, 'Wow, this guy played everything.' All my older brothers and sisters liked James Gang, Sly And The Family Stone, Hendrix, Vanilla Fudge... Maybe it was mainstream stuff, but they were hippies. I liked the soulful and ripping stuff and Zeppelin, too. I saw Grandmaster Flash and Melle Mel when they came to Seattle, but mainly I was into Prince."

It was something of a culture shock for Duff, coming to L.A. and suddenly mixing with a new type of person than he was used to in Seattle. "When I met Slash and Steve Adler for the first time," he later remembered on www.gnrsource.com, "it was weird, 'cause I'd never met guys like this before – L.A. locals. We went out that night and got drunk, and then we had this ill-fated band. It was Slash's band, Road Crew."

Like all first bands, Road Crew was anything but coherent or professional. The guys were making things up as they went along and had little idea of how things should run, let alone how to write songs. They stuck to mainly covers as their own songs were bland carbon copies of early 1980s glam rock, which was the hub of the Los Angeles music scene at the time. Duff didn't want to fall into the Seattle trap of being a musician going nowhere with a faceless, unambitious band. He wanted to hit the big time, not just scrape by as a band on the periphery of the renowned L.A. scene. Unbeknownst to Slash or Steven, Duff was viewing adverts in the music section of the local press – hoping that somewhere he could find a band with an appropriate vision.

The two musicians he came across would alter Slash's life forever. Plying their trade in a local band known as Axl were guitarist Jeffrey Dean Isbell, aka Izzy Stradlin, and singer William Bailey, aka W. Axl Rose. Both were three years older than their future band mates and it showed in their experience. Izzy was a clever songwriter with a penchant for swaying melody and sultry rock 'n' roll. Axl was a firecracker, a red-headed Adonis with a fire in his belly to match, a typically brazen frontman, all tight-veined and supple. Their proficiency as performers came from the in-depth study of other, more experienced bands working the Sunset Strip, the rock hub of which was the Troubadour club. Axl was not arrogant enough to assume he could just walk into the scene and become its new leader. He cleverly played a backseat role in the scene for two years, soaking up things to do and not to do in order to progress. Eventually, he felt ready for a full scale assault on the scene. There were numerous local musicians from this time who associated with Rose and have since fallen by the wayside in terms of relative profile. These included David Lank, Dana Gregory, David Pyle and Mike Staggs.

During these dalliances, Axl fronted bands called Axl, then Rose and then finally Hollywood Rose. Things really perked up however when he joined up with Tracii Guns in the band L.A. Guns. Axl persuaded Tracii – a professional guitarist – to form a new outfit taking the vestiges of the Rose name along with his surname. This was an improvement on the originally mooted Heads Of Amazon or worse still, 'AIDS'. Both Tracii Guns and fellow guitarist Rob Gardner soon parted ways, leaving Axl, Duff and Izzy as a trio. A tour had been organised and two replacements were needed. The remaining members felt it would be a good idea to put their new band into the public eye and thus came the world's first sighting of the newly christened Guns N' Roses.

Duff took it upon himself to call Slash and offer him the position of guitarist while Steven was offered the drum seat. Initially Slash wanted to poach Axl for Road Crew, mainly because he didn't want to play with another guitar player. However, he was soon at ease around Izzy and the two six stringers developed a unique way of bouncing ideas off each other whilst trading rhythm and lead duties as each song required; it would prove to be a historically important partnership.

If anything, coming into contact with such a good, solid player like Izzy proved to Slash how far his own playing had come in a short time. He was more than able to hold his own with the older, more accomplished musician and that felt good. What also caused a wry smile was how myopic he'd probably been in trying to push Road Crew to bigger and better things. Firstly, Guns N' Roses benefited from the collated experience and overall game plan of each of the members and secondly, Slash had nothing to worry about with this group of guys – they were one and the same despite their personality differences. Slash and Izzy were laid-back and graceful, while Duff and Steven were mischievous and engagingly child-like. The enigmatic Axl complemented the raw musicianship with his increasingly ambitious stage performances. He mimicked the likes of Marc Bolan whilst bringing a 1980s surge of updated glam metal swagger to proceedings. Rose later quipped, "When we started, we wanted to be the coolest, sexiest, meanest, nastiest, loudest, funnest band. There was a group consciousness of rape, pillage, search, and destroy."

With this first incarnation of the beastly Guns N' Roses, the band were quickly summoned to undertake a jaunt across the United States, which was later dubbed 'The Hell Tour'. The band literally had nothing except their instruments. They were driving, sleeping and drinking in one van, which would inevitably break down on numerous occasions. When they did grace a stage, it was with the proverbial one man and his dog in attendance. Yet, the band didn't care. This was a union forged on that dreadful, demanding, exhausting series of dates. Far from detracting the band from their desire to become a bunch of world renowned rock stars, it strengthened their resolve. Though the conditions were anything but perfect, it still beat working a dead-end job or hanging around butt-fuck Indiana (both Izzy and Axl came from Lafayette, Indiana and the former would often tell future interviewers to write down, "Indiana sucks").

The tour would take them north to places such as San Francisco and Seattle. On their way to Seattle for their first gig of the tour, the van broke down, leaving them to hitch-hike to their destination. Once there – due to the lack of promotion – there was barely an audience. The band still played, only to be paid nothing afterwards. This set a precedent for the remainder of the tour, at many venues the story was the same – little or no crowd to speak of and little or no money to pay their expenses, though occasionally they received beer or food as payment. Slash later said he couldn't believe they even made it back to L.A.

The twisted logic of life on the road meant that, come the end of these ramshackle shows, Guns N' Roses were an intensely tight-knit unit with a cast-iron musical chemistry. On another positive note, the endless miles had seen many song ideas form into near-finished tracks. A momentum was gathering. It would not be long before Guns N' Roses were making waves outside of the small confines of their local clubs.

Chapter 3

STRIPPING ON SUNSET

**"WE WERE SO NOT A PART OF THE
1980S HAIR BAND SCENE."**
SLASH

Returning to Los Angeles, all five bedraggled G N' R members felt that it was good to be home. Slash, ever the optimist, didn't seem to care that dreams of hot chicks on order in every city didn't materialise. Outside of L.A., no-one knew who Guns N' Roses were and though most of the band was young, good-looking and single, there was no harem of groupies across the land. Only in L.A. did the band command a sizeable audience; Slash, like his comrades, had his fair share of female admirers in his adopted home city.

At this stage, Slash worked hard, as did G N' R as a whole. Sure, some of them variously enjoyed getting wasted – in L.A. in the 1980s *everyone* got wasted – but they were astute enough to realise they had to promote the band – party hard but work hard too. As yet unsigned, they were quickly building a ground-swell of popularity just from their incendiary live shows alone.

Slash, along with Axl and Duff, was one of the main protagonists of the Guns' promotional machine, heaping flyers on locals and exercising the word of mouth relentlessly. Guns N' Roses could talk a good game but they were able to back it up: they knew the music could speak for itself. If they could just get people to the shows, then Slash's inimitable guitar style and Axl's electric vocal histrionics would bring everyone on their side.

Like other bands in Los Angeles, G N' R were stuck in a climate of 'pay-to-play'. The local authorities had recently outlawed the placing of posters and flyers on telegraph poles, though the ever cheeky Slash, coupled with friends and bandmates, would still stick a few on everywhere he went, keeping one eye out for local law enforcement as he did. The main way to promote a band was therefore to buy your own tickets and then sell them on. If you sold them all, you had a full gig, the payment took care of itself and the club was also happy as they had a venue full of drinkers. If you couldn't sell the tickets, you'd be footing the bill for the gig, adding insult to the injury of only a handful of punters being in attendance.

Through a combination of hard promotional graft and an evolving catalogue of blistering original material, Guns N' Roses sold more tickets than most and gradually they were creating a buzz around Hollywood that other bands could only dream of. Like all their contemporaries starting off on the bottom rung, Guns N' Roses began as a band who would only get to play on Monday and Tuesday nights – the 'graveyard shift' for up and coming bands. However, their performances were so staggering that they were soon moved to Wednesdays and Thursdays. The buzz was exponential and so they quickly became eligible to play on a Friday or Saturday – even then, they never once sat on their laurels, so Friday and Saturday nights were spent walking back and forth along Sunset Strip selling up to 500 tickets for between $5 and $10 to prospective fans. This potent combination of talent and drive meant they were soon offered a weekend slot as the house band for one of Los Angeles's most influential and historic clubs, The Troubadour. Inevitably, this led to a surge of interest, from fans, from groupies, from local press and, most importantly of all, from record companies.

Even at this formative stage of their career, it was clear that here was a bunch of guys truly living out their stage personas – Slash was not merely a caricature of a Jack-and-Coke drinking guitar player with a top hat, tousled hair in his eyes – this was actually him! Except he was still living with his grandmother.

His mellow 'guardian' knew Slash was just trying to make it and recognised that he absolutely devoted himself to his craft. Despite only just approaching twenty years of age, the young Slash was already blessed with a competence and attitude of someone twice his age. Slash was the embodiment of rock 'n' roll, and a damn nice guy to boot. It is highly debatable that without Slash the band would have struggled to get off the ground in their home city, let alone further afield. Here was a player that had rock 'n' roll coursing through his veins, all the way through to his permanently wedged top hat. But Slash was no gimmick, no image driven poseur. The crowd could smell the authenticity and when he wrestled with his cheap Les Paul, the notes cascaded in sublime beauty. He could play hard or soft, slow or fast and in some cases every stylistic nuance was expressed during one song. The principle songwriters were always Slash, Izzy and Axl, with the frontman especially concentrating on lyrics. Riffs were shared between the two guitarists and the rhythmic flourishes of Duff and Steven were self-imposed. Altogether this was a true unit, but in many observers' eyes, there were undoubtedly two stars shining brighter than the rest.

Everyone, even in the early days, had a favourite and it was usually either Slash or Axl. Not surprisingly, given their opposing looks, women were pretty specific about who they wanted to lay and why, but for budding musos the choice was obvious. This was something Guns N' Roses had from their very first shows – a mature and cutting edge not shared with their fellow L.A. brethren. Other bands were sloppy and often carbon copies of the burgeoning glamsters who were receiving attention from heavy metal and hard rock magazines alike. Most other Californian bands at the time dressed and looked like women. Slash stood out a mile from his peers. There were few other mixed race hard rock musicians on the scene for one, and two, his image of top hat and frizzed hair was utterly distinctive. Whether you saw him at a distance walking down the street or up close on stage, here was the one and only Slash. His long standing nickname also helped. Everyone else had to invent their own monicker, W. Axl Rose for instance. Slash was just Slash.

The guitarist would soon be joining his band mates in a run-down town house suitably named 'The Hell House', where he could concentrate fully on his rock star ambitions. The rest of the band had been living pretty itinerant lives: "I never lived in one place for more than two months, always crashing at people's houses," Rose later explained to www.bzzt.com. "My parents would say, 'Come back home and go to college and we'll pay for it' but I would reply, 'No, I have to do this now.'"

Glam rock was enjoying a resurgence, this time drenched in more hairspray than the ozone could handle; make-up counters were suddenly swamped by queues of pretty young men asking for the 'bright pink little number'. Los Angeles has long been strange to the outsider but on the Sunset Strip in the 1980s, it was pretty fucking strange to everyone living there too. Indeed, many of the females on the scene looked more like men than the men. By contrast, Slash maintained his manly air which was to serve him well.

The crowds picked up on the authenticity of the band's performances and their assembled cast. G N' R could have been a manufactured glam 'boy band' but were nevertheless strewn together completely inadvertently, living and playing by their own rules. Their dedication also led them to play outside of the generic environments for a live band. Short of money to pay for rehearsal space, not to mention studio time, the band often had to play in friend's living rooms, whether it be for parties or simply to practice.

Many Saturday evenings were spent at a mansion in Laurel Canyon where the band played for both friends and strangers. In one-time manager Vicky Hamilton's words, "In the mid-1980's in Hollywood, the scene was very much alive. People were hanging out on the Sunset Strip just passing out flyers and promoting their bands. It kind of evolved from the punk scene of the early 1980s. All the people of that 'Big Hair' scene knew each other and supported each other's bands. Then they would go to the Rainbow Bar and Grill and hang out. G N' R were simply the best band of that era and had real talent as songwriters, players and performers. It's not surprising that G N' R were the band that everyone loved."

Slash would not be alone in his assertion that Guns were not part of this hair band scene. "We were a breakout band for the 1980s," he told *Steppin' Out*, "because we were the only band like us around," he has said. "I think that is what made us so popular. We hit a certain nerve that nobody else was really doing. When the 1980s came and went, we were so out of the loop as far as trends go. It never really mattered to me or any of the other guys what anybody else was doing. We just listened to the music. We never cared about being in a popularity contest with anyone. We just did what we did good. It's not about being in a contest."

This was indicative of Slash's refreshing attitude and it is one which contributed to his success. Where everyone else was strutting their stuff arrogantly in their mother's high heels, Slash was dressing as he always had, in jeans, t-shirt and cowboy boots – the embodiment of cool. And there were no rivals as he saw it. Here was a man who could never be described as conceited, yet he knew his talents and realised Guns N' Roses was a special unit.

★ ★ ★

The 'Hell House', so christened by Izzy, was essentially a garage that doubled as a rehearsal and living space, not unlike the scene one surveys on the *Appetite For Destruction* back cover. The band later admitted living at the house was something akin to a living hell, and Izzy could often be found sleeping behind the couch for days at a time. Axl once explained the band lived on just $3.75 a day, "which was enough to buy gravy and biscuits at Denny's Deli for a buck and a quarter and a bottle of Nighttrain for a buck and a quarter or some Thunderbird. That was it. You survived."

There were regular and ongoing parties which would last for days at a time. Whenever there were girls around, which was most of the time, the unsuspecting female would sometimes have their purses raided for some much needed sustenance money!

Steven Adler: "We had all kinds of strippers coming in, and they made good money," he told www.snakepit.org. "At the start, we all had odd jobs, but then we started playing clubs and getting in to the studio, and the house became this disgusting mess. We were in a band and we got to meet girls. We never hurt nobody. One of the strippers I still know to this day, she's a lovely girl, they all really wanted to help us and that's what the lifestyle was. Really, they were the best days, just playing in the clubs, selling them out, having guys come up in the street and say, 'Hey I saw you guys, your band really kicks it!' Having girls and some pot, that was the best of it."

Musically, Guns' early material "Kicked ass!" according to Steven Adler. "We really fuckin' rocked and we meant it! The first time Axl ever rehearsed with us, we were playing in this little room. We were playing 'Reckless Life' and he fucking ran in to the room and grabbed the microphone and started screaming – really fucking screaming – and he was running literally halfway up the walls from side to side across the room. I was just kind of looking at Slash. Hell, the next morning I woke up and we had a rock 'n' roll band."

By the end of 1985, Guns N' Roses was perhaps the hottest band in the L.A. scene. With their dedication and intense live shows, Guns N' Roses might not always play the most flawless gig but there would always be a sense of excitement in the air. Interestingly, their huge audience in L.A. comprised of all the different genres that were around – old school rock 'n' roll people, punks, Beverly Hills High School teeny boppers, model chicks, drug dealers, "it was great," recalled Slash.

With public excitement on the ground reaching fever pitch, the music press inevitably became involved, which in turn led to several record companies showing an interest. Local magazine *Music Connection* was one of two or three who took an early notice of Guns N' Roses, way back during their formative series of regular Thursday nights at the Troubadour. Others, such as *Scratch* and *L.A. Rocks* helped the group transcend the insular glam and metal scene, taking them across town to potential fans who were not remotely interested in the current hair metal picture, instead still being ensconced in a post-punk music revival.

These punks would not be seen dead cruising the Sunset strip, but with help from these magazines, many realised that Guns N' Roses was in fact the first band out of the secular L.A. groupings with any originality or street vibe. It is a credit to the band that they could cross such strict boundaries in the early days without even trying. There was no pretence or pouting for the audience, it was real, concentrated and powerful.

The essential element that pricked the ears of the business-minded concert attendees was the set of terrific songs the band had created. Interspersed with covers such as Rose Tattoo's 'Nice Boys (Don't Play Rock N' Roll)' and Aerosmith's 'Mama Kin', were their own fierce compositions. Despite some of this material being in its early stages, it still sounded impressive; notably, it ran more deeply in subject matter than the other local bands ideas of 'songs' which usually centred around the sizes of their dicks, and how many girls they'd conquered the weekend before.

Guns' brand of psycho-maniac rock 'n' roll was

evident early on in the likes of 'Reckless Life', 'Shadow Of Your Love', 'Nightrain', 'Move To The City', and the seminal 'Welcome To The Jungle'. Admirably predicting the tidal wave of success which would later engulf the band, *Music Connection* took the unprecedented step of putting them on its front cover, which was the first time in the magazine's 25-year history that an unsigned band had made its front page. It was prophetic journalism at its very best. By the time the publication hit the stands, Guns N' Roses were signed to the Geffen label.

They had already released their own record by this time which was titled *Live ?!*@ Like a Suicide*, a 10,000 pressing of a collection of covers and originals that was on the fictitious Uzi Suicide label. Coupled with their take on Rose Tattoo and Aerosmith were songs such as 'Move To The City' and 'Reckless Life', tracks that were pivotal to Guns' growing stature. The band didn't feel, however, that the 'live' recording was exactly representative. As Axl surprisingly admitted, "That's the most contrived piece of shit we've done yet. It ain't a live record, if you think it is you're crazy. What we did was go into a room, record ourselves and put 50,000 screaming people on top."

Still, the 10,000 copies were snapped up by L.A. gig

veterans and other Americans hot on the pulse of the underground glam scene. This convinced a number of labels in the Hollywood area to wine and dine the band in the hope of securing their signatures. It was the Geffen team of Tom Zutaut and Teresa Ensensat who won the group over with an insistence that they would be able to do things their own way – on March 25, 1986, the band inked the deal. Finding a suitable manager proved to be more difficult however. In the past year, Guns had been helped by Vicky Hamilton, chief cheerleader and adopted mother who let the band stay with her and generally helped them out. At the time she was a booker and promoter working with Faster Pussycat and Poison as well as G N' R.

With various unexpected developments occurring in the Guns' camp, the management situation altered. "When the band first started, the image that Geffen had of us was drunken, fucked up rabble rousers and they would do anything to make that image keep going," Duff McKagan recalled a decade after the band had been signed by the company. It was something pertinent to McKagan given his condition at the time – he was reportedly drinking plentiful amounts of vodka each day and using cocaine too. He was not alone in his substance indulgence. Where Axl and Izzy seemed to be altogether less excessive, Slash, Steven and Duff were becoming embroidered in a tapestry of narcotic abuse.

Though Slash was always secretive about the amount he was consuming, he seemed to never be without a bottle of Jack, he smoked constantly and behind the scenes he was also beginning to use cocaine. "A bottle a day for five years, that's what I was doing..." Slash later said of Jack Daniels. As was characteristic, he made light of his addiction, quipping "you have really bad breath in the morning – you know, you can't have sex in the morning till you've brushed your teeth, which is a real fucking drag".

Regarding cocaine, he would explain some years down the line, "I just liked coke. I liked the way it felt. And fuck, I didn't know if I did it four or five days in a row I'd get fucking hooked on it! And that's a different subject altogether. That drug takes you over mentally and physically, so much that to come back is hard. I had not so much a drinking problem as to just want to drink and get rowdy."

Steven Adler remembers the early days, speaking to one magazine: "We'd go out and meet chicks – older women – who would take us back to their Beverly

Hills homes. They'd give us booze, coke; they'd feed us, really. All we had to do was fuck them."

One legendary music biz manager saw Guns N' Roses run up a $450 drinks tab in his name (after he had gone to bed), after which he decided against working with the band. Alan Niven eventually signed the band on behalf of Stravinsky Brothers Management.

By this time, the band had such gems as 'Sweet Child O' Mine', 'Welcome To The Jungle' and 'Paradise City' in their arsenal. Equally their inimitable attitude and built-in superiority to their peers meant the public were bound to lap up the Guns' brand of entertainment. The crop of hair bands was lame, derivative and embarrassingly in love with themselves. Repetitive tales of parties, strippers and loose women crammed their lyrics and were ubiquitous among the rock fraternity, especially those bands who believed in their own immortality and contained a strange sense of arrogance despite looking like transvestites at a jumble sale. Whereas groups such as Twisted Sister took the humourous approach to being made-up to look like unappealing women, doused in make-up and bad spandex, there were thousands of others who were deadly serious.

Guns N' Roses were certainly way ahead of their

time. Their songs also contained tales of strippers, prostitutes and girlfriends as well as the requisite drink and drug excess but it was not presented in a crass or predictable fashion. There was more bitterness, frustration, resentment, anger and anarchy than your average hair band. By examining the lyrics of their forthcoming debut album, *Appetite For Destruction* – compared to any of the equivalent records of the time – it is clearly no surprise as to why G N' R achieved the massive success they did.

Many bands were open in admitting they only started a group to get chicks. You can't say that distinction did not apply to Slash and Co., but the Guns' members were at least serious about their music and they played with their heart and soul, not their dicks. Ultimately, this is why Guns N' Roses was about to succeed on a massive scale and happily leave the other L.A. bands behind to rot in the gutter.

Chapter 4

WE GOT YOUR DISEASE

**"WHEN OUR RECORD COMES OUT, I KNOW IT'S
GOING TO BE REALLY DIFFERENT – WHETHER
IT'S ACCEPTED OR NOT I COULDN'T GIVE A SHIT."**
SLASH

Guns N' Roses were already looking far past their City of Angels horizons. A small series of dates was booked in the UK to help spread the gospel in the country of The Beatles. It was the start of a very volatile relationship with the island. The English press thrived on the arrival of the self-proclaimed 'Most dangerous band in the world'. In a surprising attack of conservatism, they anticipated five brash young Americans were here to fuck their daughters and generally pillage every town in Great Britain. The perception of Slash was the most inaccurate – most papers could not even get his name right. Some called him Slosh (which might have been appropriate given his predilection for Jack Daniels), others referred to him as

Slog or Slug. But the most hilarious perception was the false claim that he had been on a drinking binge for two years and faced each morning with hands that "shook like windmills," in his "own words." Actually, he would often comment to the music press that he had everything under control. "I really don't feel that I have the intense addiction people believe," he once rationalised.

Some publications managed to get his name right but even when Slash was name-checked correctly, the stories about the band were equally outlandish. Like the Sex Pistols before them and the Beastie Boys after, Guns N' Roses were perfect fodder for tabloid hysteria – and fabrication. One daily paper quoted Axl as saying that he liked to kill small dogs, especially those such as poodles. "Everything about them means I must kill them," he supposedly spouted, confusing rock 'n' roll animal lovers everywhere and giving Guns N' Roses the unjustifiable distinction of being unwanted in England – a nation of dog lovers, after all – before they even arrived.

A more considered distaste came from a sizeable portion of rock fans unimpressed with many American magazine claims that this band was the future for hard rock. Guns N' Roses were booked into the legendary Marquee club in London for three successive shows which seemed a little presumptuous. Of course, the management were just trying to maximise a trip to England's shores and to kick-start their profile there. The truth was that there simply weren't enough fans (yet) to make three shows sell out. It had all started well enough. Axl spouted words of warm welcome when the band first placed its collective feet on an English stage. "It's great to be in fuckin' England finally," he said. Then the atmosphere darkened. In hindsight, it seems ridiculous but when G N' R first came to the UK, they were met with a barrage of beer cups and spit, much to Axl's annoyance. Had the band's assumptions and those around them been too wayward, or was this just a typical reaction of the British crowd? It did not sit well with Axl who called one audience member a "pussy" after they had thrown a glass into Steven's drum kit on the opening night. He threatened to leave the stage if people didn't stop throwing things. Other than a free trip to merry old England, the band felt they had accomplished little with their initial visit to British shores and were unenthusiastic about returning to the country.

Besides, they had a trump card on their side – the debut album, *Appetite For Destruction*. Remarkably, the record faced mixed reviews upon its release on July

31, 1987. Some rock institutions like *Kerrang!* greeted it like a fabulous new friend. The review in issue 151 gasped, "Rock 'n' roll is being wrestled from the hands of the bland, the jaded, the tired, the worn, and thrust back into the hands of the real raunch rebels." Other publications were not so praiseworthy. *Rolling Stone*, for instance, initially distanced itself from the Guns' brand of heavy metal and would be one of the magazines most opposed to following the rush for Guns' attention.

Such critical mixed blessings mattered not. Produced by Mike Clink, the easy-going legend (who had previously worked with Ozzy Osbourne and Survivor), *Appetite For Destruction* belied the initial media indifference by becoming one of the biggest selling albums of all-time.

Somehow, the band and production team had managed to capture the G N' R's onstage intensity. Even the portraits of the band members on the album's back cover were perfectly representative of their individual contributions. There was the reflective Axl, frontman extraordinaire, carefully holding a bottle of beer in one hand, his other hand caressing his hip, bandana astride his tilted head suggesting he was deep in thought even while the photo was being taken; Izzy is quietly reflective, looking pensive as he grasps an acoustic guitar; Duff, another member to be clutching alcohol, sits looking resolutely wasted, hair slung back in wanton disarray; Slash takes the conclusion of a rebel rousing band of alcoholics to suitable depths, staring blankly through a haze of unkempt hair, top hat and bottle between his legs – happy enough. Steven sits, carefully holding bongos looking every bit the young mischievous pretty boy of the band – all girly blond hair and baby features.

The music simply underlined the respective personalities of the band members, being as brash and carefree as it was heartfelt and serious. Beginning with a Slash lick, the opening to 'Welcome To The Jungle' was one of the finest ways to begin an album, with a guitar intro that would soon be regarded as a rock classic. Of course the songs were flawless. Axl's vocals were highly distinctive and unusual but for this author, the power of the material was in the guitars. It is not stretching the truth to claim that without the Slash six-string attack, *Appetite For Destruction* would have been a very different record.

The backing refrains of the Slash and Izzy rhythm partnership carried the verse and bridge of the opening number while Axl screamed and teased his vocals. The main guitar solo was relatively simple yet ultimately memorable, a prominent feature in the early work of Slash. He did not try and cram in as many notes as possible for the sake of it, like many of his more self-indulgent peers. Other 1980s American high-brow guitarists had been trained at the 'posh' Guitar Institute Of Technology (or G.I.T. for short) whereas Slash, of course, had taught himself everything he knew. This gave him a simple sense of feel many other musicians lacked and it is this heartfelt character which lifts *Appetite...* beyond the norm.

In fairness, every member of the band contributed something unique which collectively is what makes the album so special. Yet, even in their unity, there was a friendly opposition which also raised the bar for Guns' material. The differences in Slash and Izzy's playing were obvious. Never more so than on the laid-back soft rock of 'It's So Easy' or 'Think About You'. Slash was on fire in the more aggressive material such as 'You're Crazy' and 'Out Ta Get Me' and it was on songs such as this where Slash and Axl's partnership sprang into top gear.

Steven And Duff held the band together with a superglue rhythm section and Izzy was a mean song writer and rhythm player but, for the author, the stars of

Appetite For Destruction were Slash and Axl. They didn't know it at the time, but they had just sealed themselves into the rock 'n' roll hall of fame. The last true guitarist/vocalist partnership that mattered had been Steven Tyler and Joe Perry of Aerosmith. Prior to that there was Page and Plant, the Led Zeppelin maestros and of course, Rolling Stones' Jagger and Richards. The press loved these combinations, stating that every great rock 'n' roll band needed the chalk and cheese of an electric lead player and lead singer. Even now, writing in the 21st century, the last great rock partnership of this type is *still* Slash and Axl. This is just one mark of proof that here was an exceptional coupling.

Yet, despite the duo's brilliance, there was no grand design from either man. They had not contrived to form a legendary partnership – which was one reason why it worked so well. The chemistry – and conversely the acidity – is what made it a truly remarkable association. Slash couldn't help the way he looked but in being so unusual for the rock world, mixed race with afro hair and a top hat, he instantly drew attention to himself. And no-one can ignore a good frontman. Put the two together and you had the leaders of Guns N' Roses and each played their role to perfection.

Tension between Slash and Axl was inevitable given that Slash was laid-back, friendly and easy-going while Axl had a volatility and combativeness about him. The singer had long been both a close friend as well as a mystery to his band mates. Slash once talked of how Axl could be a difficult character, then turn around and be "the nicest guy in the world". This was an opinion that many people who came into contact with Axl Rose seemed to share. An enigma, a legend, a firebrand.

Every song on *Appetite...* was different, from the energetic bursts of 'Anything Goes' and 'My Michelle', to the more subdued refrains of 'Rocket Queen' and 'Nightrain'. The latter symbolised the creative nuances of the Guns' repertoire. Produced and mixed expertly, the two differing guitar parts during the verse come out of alternate speakers and add to the overall effect, before climaxing in a crescendo of syncopatic rhythm for the chorus.

'Rocket Queen' was a climactic album closer in more ways than one. Where all but one track ('Paradise City') were spliced together in roughly three or four minutes and thus primed for radio, the end track was something of a jam. Yet it symbolised the versatility of the band, sounding almost at odds with the rest of the material. There were even authentic squeals of orgasmic delight from a girl fucked in the studio and recorded during her climax.

But the real jewel in the crown of *Appetite For Destruction* was the love torn ballad, 'Sweet Child O' Mine' (originally the lyrics formed a love letter to Axl's then-girlfriend Erin Everly) which has become as famous for the Slash intro riff as for the song itself. The high-pitched beginning initially was a joke by Slash, something he would often play as a warm-up exercise when rehearsing alone. Then one day, he hit the notes in front of Steven and played the tune he referred to as 'circus-like' while pulling funny faces at the drummer. Steven asked him to play the riff again, at which point Izzy's ears pricked and he found the appropriate backing chords. Though Slash was anything but convinced this was an ideal song introduction, everyone else persuaded him it was something special. For a long time Slash viewed the intro with disdain but ultimately conceded it was "okay". Of course, the track has since gone down in musical history as one of the greatest songs of all-time.

"That's just my 'pick up a guitar and fuck around with it' style of playing," Slash would shrug when talking to *Guitar World*. "The riff started out as a stupid exercise that I noodled around with nearly every time I picked up a guitar. I don't really know how to practice properly, so I like to make up things that are difficult to play, so that I can become better at what I do. I must have played that riff a million times."

This tune has ranked highly in numerous charts for 'Greatest Song Ever' but just as many music journalists have seen fit to place the guitar introduction just as high. Indeed, in a poll for the magazine *Guitar World,* the solo ranked at #37 in the reader's poll for the Top 100 'Greatest Guitar Solos of All-time'.

The album was littered with memorable introductions of one kind – be it the soft jangling beginning to 'Paradise City' or the bubbling tom tom hurl of the opening bars of 'Mr Brownstone'. The choruses were just as strong and the album was chock full of choice singles. Initially the choice of 'Welcome To The Jungle' and 'Sweet Child O' Mine' didn't set the world on fire but when the stated brilliance of the album filtered around the world the singles were re-released and so Guns N' Roses ascent began.

The band had a secret weapon in the cover art for *Appetite For Destruction.* Drawn by fantasy artist Robert Williams, the scene featured a nefarious robotic creature leering over a half-naked woman with her underwear pulled down wickedly low. It was open to interpretation what had happened to the woman with a bare breast on show and a look of unerring horror on her face.

Stores across the US were appalled and many refused to carry the offending sleeve. Likewise, the prim and proper chain stores in England such as W H Smiths also turned away the album. It was not enough for the record to include more f-words than the average PMRC advocate would despair of; this record was positively offensive in its audacity and luridness and so the cover art was quickly censored.

There was a thank you credit for the actress and musician Christina Veronica, Slash's girlfriend at the time. Later, there would be a published photograph showing the two in bed together. Veronica peaks over the covers, unaware she was being snapped. It was a photo she would later claim embarrassed her. Slash was, as ever, unconcerned.

The whole package for the debut album was awesome in its execution. However, aside from the controversial artwork, away from the image of the band and the speculation about their hedonistic lifestyles, there was at the core a historically significant collection of songs.

SLASH

Each track deserved its place and stature befitting one of the greatest records of all-time. Twelve tracks, twelve stunning choruses, a scattering of memorable guitar licks and solos crunched together to create a sound that has barely dated in twenty years.

Chapter 5

BEFORE THE HANGMAN'S NOOSE

**"THE FIRST TIME I TOOK HEROIN I KNEW
I'D DISCOVERED [SOMETHING] . . . I NEVER LIKED
THE HYPED-UP STATE COCAINE PUTS YOU IN."**
SLASH

In their early days of existence, Guns N' Roses were always on the edge, hanging on a precipice of rock 'n' roll excess. Slash and Izzy were the quiet double team responsible for a sizeable part of the band's success – each was always able to play guitar like a man possessed and it always sounded great. Axl Rose was not so lucky. For one, in being the singer he was more liable to problems with his particular instrument, in addition to which the frontman had already had more than his fair share of problems with ailments.

"I've had a mutated form of polio, a mutated form of rubella, the swine flu, scarlet fever, and strep throat in my heart," Axl told *RIP*. "It's mostly respiratory stuff. Air conditioners in hotels circulate the same air, and on the plane everyone's breathing the same air. So if anyone's got anything, my tonsils grab it. That's one of the reasons I've never liked touring."

Slash was ultimately a happy guy, thankful for his opportunities in life and able to take advantage of a chance when it presented itself. Saul Hudson was always in control, even in moments of excess. Having an often vexed and fiery friend and frontman by his side, however, frequently troubled his equilibrium. He would tell magazines how he respected Axl and thought his contribution to G N' R was unparalleled – honest feelings too – but deep down, the seeds were being sown for a final confrontation between the two.

When the band were playing a show in Atlanta, police stormed the stage to arrest Axl following an earlier incident with a security guard just before the band went on. Guns had just warmed up and were into their second song of the set when the melee happened. The remaining members were dismayed but carried on as a four piece. There followed a hurried improvisational scenario where Slash and Steven played a fifteen-minute and ten minute solo respectively (not to mention the rather awkward debuting of a roadie on vocals!) Axl received a warning from police and was then free to go; the band were garnering attention for the wrong reasons and tensions were starting to fester beneath the surface.

They were instantly buoyed by news of a very special invitation however. Guns N' Roses were touted to tour England with America's (and their own) favourite rock 'n' roll band, Aerosmith. However at the last minute Aerosmith pulled out and G N' R were faced with either touring alone or finding a hasty replacement. The band chose to take Faster Pussycat on the road with them – still the tour was not without incident. Steven Adler broke his hand in a street fight and Cinderella's Fred Coury had to to step in to take over the drum seat.

The bands played at prestigious venues such as the Hammersmith Odeon in London and the Manchester Apollo, instantly justifying their new-found fame by captivating the larger theatres. In Manchester, however, ticket sales were not quite as glorious as might have been expected, despite Geffen having just released 'Welcome To The Jungle' as a single. The Apollo theatre had its upper balcony cordoned off and it was therefore a more subdued show that ran at only just over the hour. In Nottingham, the reaction was more fanatical and Axl responded in kind. The band played with such gusto they had the hundreds of Rock City regulars stamping their feet in rebellious bravado, lasting the full two hours of the band's live show, including the encores which threatened to boil the crowd into shadows of steam. Fans then gathered on the quiet Nottingham streets and almost pushed the Guns' tour bus on its head as it tried to weave its way out of the confines of a dreary English winter evening.

The English press reacted as impassibly as before, speaking in derisory tones of a band supposedly on the verge of collapse, with words like 'volatile' and 'temperamental' being used liberally to define Axl's personality – it seemed England wasn't big enough for Guns N' Roses.

This made little difference. By the time of their final show in the UK, at the Hammersmith Odeon, a venue immortalised by metal legends such as home-grown favourites Iron Maiden, the band almost sold out the venue and took it upon themselves to play their longest set of the tour, clearly enjoying the rapturous reception. They underlined their desire to do their own thing by playing for shorter periods when the crowd did not suit them or were not vociferous enough – as in Manchester – to revelling in their status if the attendant throng embraced them more readily, as in London. Fairly swiftly, a sold-out fanatical crowd was the norm. Their live reputation was handsomely rewarded when the Guns had the unprecedented honour of being chosen as the band to join Motley Crue on a tour of the States. The momentum notched up another gear.

The fast-rising popularity of the band was difficult for its members to deal with but for some years afterwards they seemed to ride the wave unerringly and simply go with the flow, without realising the effect it was having on them. Duff, reminiscing in *Classic Rock* in 2003, commented, "Back when the band started, we all came from humble backgrounds. We got our first cheques for forty grand and it was like, 'Whoa!' We'd been living on a hundred bucks a week. None of us had seen anything close to that before. Then the next cheque came, and then the really big cheques came, and they just kept coming."

Unbeknownst to the other members at the time, Axl had quickly developed a business sense that would soon land him with the dubious honour of 'leader of the band'. For all intents and purposes, they were a collection of ragamuffins when they joined Motley Crue around America. Living out a dream which had seemed too wild to comprehend even a year ago, the band was now part of something it could not fully control. The merger of two such excess hungry groups of vagabonds was bound to create interest and frenzied anticipation ... as well as incident.

Though Slash would state that his indulgences were under control, it seemed he would often get involved with those who weren't so careful. One New Year's Eve at 7pm, Slash called a friend saying he was ensconced in a hotel with Motley Crue's Nikki Sixx. Nikki had announced at one stage he was going to another room to find his guitar for an impromptu jam; a full hour later, Slash realised that Nikki hadn't actually come back. Opening the door on his way to find the lanky bassist, Slash tripped over the numb, blue body of Nikki Sixx. Like a scene from a bad rock 'n' roll movie, Sixx had overdosed. Thankfully, Nikki Sixx made it through. There were other incidents involving not only overdoses but also general debauchery, as you might expect. The fact that Sixx's heart had actually stopped for a full two minutes was immortalised in the Crue song, 'Kickstart My Heart' which appeared later on their *Dr Feelgood* album.

On stage, Guns N' Roses were gradually usurping their touring partners – and other fellow rockers – in terms of excess, in-fighting and most importantly, popularity. The fact that Axl was arrested (at the L.A. Cathouse, for leaping into the crowd and fighting with a security guard who was harassing one of the band's friends) only served to highlight his, and Guns' notoriety.

Things would never be the same again.

Chapter 6

BE THE BALL

"MY PEERS SUCK. THEY'RE REALLY BAD. I HOPE THAT IN ANOTHER
FIVE YEARS GUNS N' ROSES ISN'T CONSIDERED ANOTHER POISON OR KINGDOM
COME. I HOPE WE'RE REMEMBERED AS BEING DIFFERENT. I MEAN WE'RE
IN A BAD TIME FOR ROCK 'N' ROLL NOW … PEOPLE JUST AREN'T DOING
ANYTHING FROM THEIR SOUL. I WOULD HOPE THAT WE'RE A BIT AWAY FROM
THAT AS FAR AS THE MUSIC GOES."
SLASH

One reason Guns N' Roses achieved legendary status so quickly was their legendary pairing with rock behemoths Aerosmith, after the latter offered them a support slot on a full US tour. Though Guns were influenced by the band and somewhat star-struck by their invitation, the 'Smith actually had a fair helping of respect and admiration for the Gunners and thus, a perfect partnership was formed.

First up, however, the band performed on Fox network's *The Late Show* and hinted at their ambitious new material. They played an acoustic version of 'You're Crazy' and also a song which was used as a future b-side, 'Used To Love Her' – a humorous tale of burying an ex-girlfriend. Slash pointed out that everyone who heard the song usually found it funny except those without a sense of humour. Axl himself later explained in sleeve notes that the song should be taken as nothing more than a joke.

Slash said of 'You're Crazy': "It's a lot bluesier (sic), which is the way me and Axl and Izzy originally wrote it. I think I prefer the slower version, it's got something. I don't know but every time we play it in that slower style, something weird happens, something magical. We've never done it the same way twice."

Aerosmith manager Tim Collins, quoted in the Aerosmith book *Walk This Way*, said of the G N' R tour announcement, "… we needed a great opening act for the summer shows and [someone] suggested Guns N' Roses. I said 'We can't do this. We're sober, they've [got] heroin users and drug addicts.' But he insisted we find a way to handle this so we came up with a plan."

That plan involved Guns N' Roses limiting their use of drugs or alcohol to the confines of their own dressing room which seemed fair to all involved. Besides, it wasn't the first time Aerosmith had issued such regulations to support bands. Guns N' Roses were felt to be a whole different type of band, however, and the revelation that Aerosmith's men in control had been clearing all bars containing alcohol before they arrived might have scared the Gunners had they known the exact nature of the band's concern.

However, this was simply too good an opportunity to pass up. It might also have been assumed by fans of both Guns N' Roses and Aerosmith that each band could handle such a tour without the use of narcotics. Slash would later say in *Kerrang!* "Aw, man, it was great... some funny shit went down on that Aerosmith tour. We were so similar, and yet we made such a contrast. They're all 'straight' now; clean. And their whole operation runs like clockwork; they stay in one place for four or five gigs, then when the tour moves a little further up the road they move to another place and make that their base for the next five gigs, or whatever. The whole thing is kept well under control which is exactly the opposite, of course, from the way we usually get things done. We travel the whole time, and very little of what we do is done, uh, straight..."

Tim Collins told *BAM* about the stipulation regarding Guns' alcohol and narcotics use. "We made a deal with them. We told them we wouldn't pay for any of their drugs or alcohol – we didn't want to enable their activities," he explained. "But if they chose to use drugs they could do that in their dressing room. At the beginning it worked so well that the bands had no contact, but it gradually loosened up and the Gunners were respectful and everyone got along great."

Slash did however explain that Guns were still able to do their own thing. He said, "They were exposed to us the whole time, and we got to hang out together a lot which was really cool, because those guys have all been heroes of mine since I was a kid and first started listening to rock 'n' roll." And as for drinking away from their presence, it was not a problem, though Slash did concede that he used a cup to drink his Jack Daniels from. Aerosmith were no pious preachers given their new found sobriety and it seemed the members of Guns were more concerned with how Aerosmith would react to their activities than Aerosmith themselves were.

On one occasion, Steven Tyler came into a room that Slash used for tuning his guitar. While Slash was out of the room, Tyler was inquisitively looking through his tapes. There was one empty and one half-empty bottle of Jack lying around. Slash walked back in and Tyler said, 'Did you drink all that today?' When the G N' R guitarist said, 'Yes', Tyler he just gave him a look.

Tyler was complimentary about his supporting band to every magazine he spoke to. "What got me is they were us," he quipped. "The bass player *is* Tom Hamilton, Slash *is* Joe Perry, Izzy *is* Brad and the drummer is that close to Joey Kramer. Axl is the same as me, a visionary egomaniac. Sometimes I walked into their dressing room and it was like looking in a mirror. I talked to them a little about drugs. Aerosmith was upset that the press was giving us a lot of shit about supposedly not letting them drink and smoke and do drugs. That offended us because we never presumed to tell anyone that. Before the first show I got Izzy – who I once did drugs with – and Slash and maybe Duff to come to my dressing room. I told them where I came from with drugs and booze." They were okay, they told us we were their idols. We had shirts printed up with the names of the rehabs we had gone through instead of tour dates and we gave them to the guys in Guns. That was our statement."

Slash maintained a vibe offstage and off-tour that underlined both his and G N' R's respect for Aerosmith but also their desire to overtake them as kings of rock. He was quoted as saying on one hand that he felt like a kid again when he had watched old footage of Aerosmith playing in 1975 which reminded him why he wanted to be a musician; yet he also suggested Guns N' Roses were the best placed band to take that mantle, some thirteen years later.

"We filled a void which someone had left a long time ago," he said in one interview. "Aerosmith used to do, I think, what we do. But even Aerosmith isn't the same thing any more. Even though they're still around, because they're older and experienced, been through the mill and this and that, they're on another plateau now where they're not going to fill that gap that they left. So along come these guys, us right? And we're just going for it."

Of course, Guns' live shows were now a must-attend event, even for their elders. Aerosmith often watched the youngsters from the side of the stage, marvelling at how quickly the rag-tag ensemble had progressed. Slash gushed of receiving praise from the 'Smith frontman. "I did a guitar solo one night – one of those finger picking slow blues things – and after the show, Tyler got me to one side and said, 'That was amazing!'" he remembered. "I just stood there and said, 'Well, thanks', and couldn't think of anything else to say. I was blown away. Seriously, that's something I'll never forget."

While the bands co-existed quite happily, Guns' burgeoning success threatened to outshine the headliners. Tim Collins said, "By the end of the tour, Guns N' Roses were huge. They basically just exploded. We were all pissed that *Rolling Stone* showed up to do a story on Aerosmith but Guns N' Roses ended up on the cover of the magazine. Suddenly the opening act was bigger than we were!

We felt sorry for them. They were so fucked up it was ridiculous … They were travelling like gypsies their old suitcases held together by twine and gaffer tape. At the end of the tour we bought them all new Halliburton cases …"

The most ramshackle famous band in the world had a guitarist who was still living out of a suitcase, staying in hotels in L.A. It was only later that year that Slash actually bought himself an apartment in North Hollywood. The abode was five minutes drive from The Roxy, The Rainbow and a whole host of other dingy clubs and bars he liked to visit. "I can't live off everybody else forever; if I can afford to have a place," he thought. "I can't just keep being, like, a total fuckin' gypsy all my life."

★   ★   ★

Gruelling though their live schedule was, Guns N' Roses were already looking to the next record. Slash explained that he had already started writing for the follow-up to *Appetite For Destruction*. He used an eight-track mobile studio to put down the best ideas on tape.

For Slash, his dishevelled appearance belied his strong work ethic and it was a surprise to some that he actually worked on the band all the time and maintained a highly productive schedule.

A typical day for the guitarist involved waking early, around 8:30 or 9:00 in the morning, visiting the Geffen Records office and handling the G N' R press, everything from interviews to promotional activities. "One morning they woke me up at 5:30a.m. to talk to some guy on the phone from a magazine in Greece," Slash explained. "But that's not every day. And it's a small price to pay, anyway – for not having to worry about your rent, and getting to work on time every day, and all these other horrors that our music has helped us escape. To pay for those privileges, you have to fuckin' be there for the few responsibilities you do have as a band member."

It was a typically humble statement from Slash and it showed his dedication to his fans and his art. As he also added, "Anybody can sit around all day just getting out of their heads... and I should know. I'm still not very good at looking after myself in lots of ways, but I take the best care of my music I can, and my music takes care of me." This exposed a rare humility and application that was perhaps surprising within the context of such an extravagant band.

BE THE BALL

The media regularly questioned relations between Axl and Slash but there seemed to be an invisible bond that glued them together. Slash would comment, "The relationship between most lead singers and most lead guitar players is very sensitive, very volatile – I could go on listing these things for hours. It's just very intense. It has major ups and major downs. But somewhere between all this intensity and this friction, there's *chemistry*. And if the chemistry's right, like Axl and me are really tight, then there's something – a spark or, you know, a need, that holds it together. You fight too. The biggest fights are between me and Axl but that's also what makes it happen."

Guns N' Roses were turning into a global phenomenon. This was proven when they were invited to play the Monsters Of Rock Festival at Castle Donington in Leicestershire, England. Though they were essentially a new band, their status was such that they were placed higher up the bill than any other newcomer would have normally reached. And on the day itself, a huge contingent of Guns fans paid on the gate to watch their new heroes. Donington 1988 was the biggest ever attendance for the festival, reaching well over 100,000 people. There were roughly 35,000 who bought tickets on the day – it is without a doubt that many of those extra fans came because of Guns N' Roses, plus the fact that the bill itself was arguably the strongest in Donington's history. Along with the aforementioned acts were Megadeth and Kiss.

It was not without some carnage, however.

As G N' R took to the stage at their proposed time slot of 2pm with 'It's So Easy', fans at the front began to lose their footing in the masses of mud. Midway through the semi-acoustic version of 'You're Crazy', Axl wisely announced to the crowd that they needed to calm down, given the conditions underfoot, but it seemed his pleas fell on deaf ears. As the band launched into 'Paradise City', the throng of bodies looked to be in even more danger. Axl breathlessly pleaded, "Look! I'm taking time out from my playing to do this and that's the only fun I get all day." The retort seemed to restrain the actions of the crowd but there were problems ahead. The band finished off with a plaintive 'Patience' before Slash announced the arrival of 'Sweet Child O' Mine' – which received the biggest cheer of the day. Axl remarked at the climax "Don't kill yourselves!"

But the damage had been done much earlier.

Two fans, twenty-year-old Landon Siggers and eighteen-year-old Alan Dick had been crushed beneath the crowd and into the mud below. The band played on unawares and the crowd didn't notice they were trampling on two of the audience. It was only at the end of G N' R's set that anyone found the two men who were rushed to the backstage emergency centre. They were pronounced dead on arrival. The body of Landon Siggers had to be identified from his tiger and scorpion tattoos on his arms, as he was otherwise unrecognisable.

★ ★ ★

A full 57 weeks after entering the US *Billboard* Top 200, *Appetite For Destruction* finally reached the top position, along with the issue of 'Sweet Child O' Mine' as a single – timed perfectly to match *Appetite For Destruction*'s success. It was now official – Guns N' Roses were the biggest rock band in the world.

Such was the frenzy of interest in the band that they had to follow up their debut record with something, so they settled on releasing their very first self-released EP, mixing it with their new acoustic numbers. That meant an extended mini-album of eight tracks which went down well with the public, as a worthy stop-gap before a full-length follow up studio album.

Titled *G N' R Lies*, the record's cover image was parodied as a newspaper front page, espousing the rumours and mostly ridiculous stories involving the band. This was the group at its most humorous, cheeky and vitriolic. Inside the record was further evidence of the band's interest in the way the British press had treated them, especially over the Donington incident. As well as a page three girl ("the loveliest girls are always in your G N' R LP") there was a reference to the popular soap *Eastenders*, with the headline, "*Westenders* star goes back to jail. Dinky Den in the pen." Not to forget the ultra English phrase, "Let the sods rot in jail!" Even the Royal family could not escape a mention with the caption, "Heir to throne caught with trousers down in lurid lust pit."

There was a sarcastic dig at those who believed Axl was the Second Coming of the Messiah, with a headline squeezed into the bottom right corner of the cover which asked, "Can Axl help you? If you've got a problem I'm here to help." The explanation to 'You're Crazy' was also a reminder of the band's attitude – it stated the song was not something that had been done for any reason other than something to amuse themselves. "We do what we want," was the conclusion.

The recording was so casual that it sounded as if

many of the second side's cuts had been recorded in one take, or at least in a very 'live' environment. You could even hear guitar picks dropping on the floor and the band members talking and counting the songs in, as with the unmistakable Duff introducing 'Patience'.

Despite the success and impression the other songs made, …*Lies* would be forever synonymous with one track in particular and that was the barrage of low slung redneck angst that was 'One In A Million'. This was a song regarding Axl Rose's first arrival in Los Angeles but he made the mistake of referring to "n★★★ers", "immigrants" and "faggots". The irony of being mixed race was not lost on Slash but the guitarist seemed to take the inevitable media furore in his stride. He was relatively tolerant of his vocalist but others – particularly the press – were not so forgiving.

Axl's use of expletives, racial and homosexual phrases did not sit well with many who couldn't quite believe their ears at hearing such words uttered calmly and forcefully on a mainstream record. Slash tried to divert unwanted attention by suggesting Axl's intentions were misunderstood, that his lyrics were merely a story of an outsider coming to the big city.

"When I use the word immigrants, what I'm talking

about is going to a 7-11 or Village pantries – a lot of people from countries like Iran, Pakistan, China, Japan etcetera, get jobs in these convenience stores and gas stations," Axl said in *Rolling Stone* wistfully. "Then they treat you as if you don't belong here. A six-foot tall Iranian with a butcher knife has chased me out of a store with Slash because he didn't like the way we were dressed. Scared me to death. All I could see in my mind was a picture of my arm on the ground, blood going everywhere. When I get scared, I get mad. I grabbed the top of one of these big orange garbage cans and went back at him with this shield, going, 'Come on!' I didn't want to back down from this guy. Anyway that's why I wrote about immigrants. Maybe I should have been more specific and said; 'Joe at the 7-11 and faggots make no sense to me.' That's ridiculous! I summed it up simply and said, 'Immigrants.'"

Deep down, however Slash was unsettled by such remarks. In many ways, the words Axl used on 'One In A Million' saw the first cracks in the previously impenetrable armour of the original G N' R.

Chapter 7

A TANGLE OF LIES

**"LOOK AT ME - T-SHIRT, JEANS, BOOTS, THAT'S ME,
THAT'S ALL THERE IS, THAT'S ALL THERE'S GONNA BE.
GIMME A ROOF OVER MY HEAD AND SOMETHING
TO DRINK AND I'VE GOT EVERYTHING I NEED. WHAT
DIFFERENCE IS THIS MONEY GOING TO MAKE?"**
SLASH

In 1989, Guns N' Roses were invited to appear at the nationally televised American Music Awards where they won the 'Favourite Rock/Pop Single' award for 'Sweet Child O' Mine'. Unfortunately, Slash and Duff had partaken in the backstage free booze to such an extent that by the time they had to take to the stage and make an acceptance speech they were so intoxicated they barely knew or cared that they publicly said "fuck" thirty times each. Geffen were incensed and immediately suggested the band, and Slash and Duff in particular, get their act together. The label was not the only party to push them into some form of action. Axl Rose himself was becoming frustrated with certain members' drug and alcohol abuse, to the extent he announced live onstage, in support of the Rolling Stones at the Los Angeles Coliseum that year, some band members should stop "dancing with Mr Brownstone". It seemed clear that he was referring directly to Slash and the guitarist did well to continue playing after such a public admonishment.

It was not as if there was any ambiguity about Slash's narcotics habit. He told *RIP* magazine that heroin was his favourite drug. He claimed to feel paranoid the police might be after him and could turn up at his door at any moment. Steven Adler explained his own situation: "Heroin was something that Slash was doing, because we came off that huge tour and we were waiting to go in to the studio ... it was just something people were doing. I don't blame my decision to try it on Slash, and I thought well, let me try it. I kind of took it to make the time go by. Getting addicted was the last thing I expected to happen."

After the band finally finished touring in support of *Appetite For Destruction*, Slash said to www.hem.passagen.se that, "When they dropped us off at the airport after the tour was over, I had nowhere to go. It kind of runs in the family with us – maybe not with Axl but definitely with me – where if I'm not busy and focused, I get loaded to pass the time. So that's what happened. I went through a phase of that and then I cleaned up and we tried to rehearse and write new material." Slash seemed somewhat perplexed. "The worst thing of it, though, was because of no longer having to live in one room, the band got separated, getting their own homes. And that was the hardest part. It's like Slash is here, Axl's here, Izzy's over there, Duff's here, and I don't even know where Steven lives, right? Like, Duff, can we come over? 'Well, the gardener is coming today...' That was a whole huge experience that really took a while for me to adjust to."

Where Adler was now involved, Slash was about to quit drugs. Several times the guitarist overdid it; at one time he was even pronounced dead, revived, then checked himself out of hospital because he had a show to play. "It's interesting that I'm still alive," he would say ten years after giving up drugs. "The drugs killed me a dozen times and for some reason they always resuscitated me. Eventually I thought, 'Somebody's trying to keep me here so I shouldn't take advantage of it so much.' That sort of slowed me down. And then I just drank myself almost to death."

"They told me I only had three months to live, if I was lucky," the guitarist later claimed. "So I cleaned myself up, got my health back, and now I just drink a glass a night. Well maybe I have a few shots and a couple of glasses of wine."

Aside from the obvious health risks, Slash also gave up the drugs because of the effect on his playing guitar. Sure, he played mightily on the Guns' studio material, but he himself knew he was not 100 percent and once it got to that stage, he returned to his playing with sober reflection. "One thing I always had was my ability to play guitar," he explained. "When I found I couldn't even do that, I knew it was time to quit, although it took me some time. I don't spend time chasing dealers around anymore. After a while that kind of lifestyle becomes a drag. For me, it became a burden and a pain in the ass rather than something that was fun and exciting, so I just stopped. As a result, I spend more time focused on guitar, and I have more energy to devote to it."

Although it did not seem apparent to the band members at the time, the last few years had taken their toll as much as they had brought success. Relationships were fragmented between the core members. What had once been a closely bonded brotherhood seemed to subside with the appearance of fame and money. It also gave certain members an appropriate method of getting regularly blitzed in order to escape the pressures of being constantly in the public eye. By contrast, while Axl thrived on the attention – like most great frontmen – those who were always shy individuals had more difficulty coping.

Therefore what was previously recreational substance use, turned into an addiction. Slash tried to rationalise his obsession by saying, "You end up drinking a lot to come out of your shell. In that way it's a vicious sort of drug because it really works."

Situations ranged from the bizarre to the ridiculous. As Slash recalled, "I lost somebody's car the other night. I borrowed a car to drive myself home from a friend's, and I parked it somewhere, but I can't remember where. It's just gone, kaput! I have the keys sitting on the table in my living room, and I don't even know where it is."

Remarkably, the adulation suddenly experienced by Slash had not gone to his head. *Kerrang!* readers voted him 'Best Rock Guitarist' which he found a proud accomplishment, but he was philosophical about life in the public eye. He said, "There are people I know that walk around believing their own hype. Then all of a sudden it turns to the next flavour of the month and they get left standing there looking on, wondering what the fuck happened."

It seemed Slash wasn't about to let the distraction of being one of the most recognisable and admired guitarists in the world stop him from being himself by becoming consumed in the rapidly escalating mythology surrounding the G N' R camp. It is in truth an attitude that remained with all the musicians in the band and perhaps is one of the reasons to explain why they are all still around; some more prominently than others.

There had been plans for Guns N' Roses to record an 'x-rated album' or another EP featuring cover versions of The Damned, Sex Pistols and other punk material, but this was to come later. Instead, the band travelled to Rumbo Studios in Canoga Park, where they had recorded *Appetite For Destruction*.

However lucid the band appeared to be at live gigs, there was one in particular, at the Hoosierdome (now the RCA Dome), where Steven Adler at least was seriously out of time with the rest of the band. It was clear he had no choice but to enter rehabilitation before work could continue on the second studio album due to be called *Use Your Illusion*. Plans for reformation were scuppered however when Steven walked out of the Bryon clinic to score drugs again. Friends became very concerned for his well-being.

Slash commented at the time in *RIP*: "When the sex and drugs and the whole bit started to get out of hand, [Steven] went right along with it … we always told each other when it was getting real bad. Everybody was there for the individual who needed help. That's how we've survived as a band." Guns N' Roses thrived on being a tight unit, a 'gang', like all the great bands before them, and their solidarity and internal chemistry are what helped them create such great music. Ultimately, however, the drug use within the band would begin to take a damaging toll. The cracks were starting to widen and with expectations on the group as high as ever, the pressure was mounting.

Unfortunately, the exact circumstances are subject to heated debate, but suffice to say, Adler was no longer in the band. He openly admits to having had issues with drugs, but argues that he was keen to make the new recordings and that he even went to the studio when he was very sick. He goes on to say that his drug battles were most serious *after* he left Guns N' Roses. "I love those guys, Guns N' Roses was always the five of us … it hurts me so bad that I didn't play on the *Use Your Illusions* …"

By contrast, Slash clearly disagrees and the bad feeling appears to still exist to this day. He has been quoted in *Circus* magazine as saying, "I lost all concern and feeling for the guy."

According to Adler, after he left the band and his health worsened, his speech was completely indecipherable for a while. All in all, he had to visit the emergency rooms of various hospitals over thirty times, by his own admission. It was a true shame to see two good childhood friends like Slash and Steven fall out for good, but as a wise man once said, "the drugs don't work, they just make you worse."

Chapter 8

LOSING MY ILLUSION

"WE TOURED FOR SO FUCKING LONG, AND BY THE TIME THE TOUR WAS
OVER WE WERE TOLD WE WERE MEGA – SPINAL TAP, YOU KNOW. 'YOU'RE
GREAT!' AND THERE'S ALL THIS STUFF GOING ON AROUND YOU, ALL THESE
PEOPLE TREATING YOU LIKE YOU'RE ON A PEDESTAL EVEN IF YOU
DON'T FEEL THAT WAY. SO WE WENT FROM NOWHERE TO BEING THIS
REALLY HUGE BAND, NOT FEELING ANY DIFFERENT, ONLY HAVING PEOPLE
TELL YOU THAT AND REACT TO YOU IN A CERTAIN WAY."
SLASH 1988

And so to one of the most gargantuan rock records of all time. 'Records' is quite apt as well, considering there were two of the bastards. *Use Your Illusion* – a title taken from a Mark Kostabi painting – was a mammoth undertaking for any rock outfit. When it was Guns N' Roses though, it was somehow expected. As ever with G N' R, there had been rumours for some time, so in actuality the public knew this was to be an ambitious double set, but they could not have predicted the sheer depth and proficiency of the songs. Was this really the same band who just four years earlier had set the world ablaze with a snotty punk metal attack? Here they were, with budget no object, utilising banjos, pianos, synthesizers, a full brass section, even a sitar. Dizzy Reed was also enlisted as a full time keyboardist.

Such grandiose ideas were unprecedented for a simple rock 'n' roll band and in truth the outlandish instrumentation did not sit well with Slash. He wasn't alone either. Izzy Stradlin was becomingly increasingly despondent with such lavish presentation. Both of the guitarists felt as if the songs were good in the first place, why did they need to be dressed up and garnished to such theatrical effect? There was only one man who could answer that and he sang the songs. *Use Your Illusion* was as much an Axl Rose release as it was Guns N' Roses. On almost every song, the frontman received a credit and it was he alone who sought a deeper sound for his band. Hard rock heroes such as Queen and middle of the road 'adult' rock such as Elton John combined in Axl's mind and he relished the chance to break out his piano.

In fairness, the overall effect of *Use Your Illusion*, which was released in two parts on the same day, was fantastic. It was certainly ambitious – some would argue verging on pretentious – but there was no arguing with the majority of the material. Many would come to believe that if the two albums had been shorn of their 'filler' tunes, then it may well have been the best rock album of all-time.

Despite some reservations, Slash would concur with that sentiment. He would later say, "*Use Your Illusion* is, to us personally, a special record. Granted there was too much material, there's too much production, there's this, that and the other, but it's a result of something that most people will never see into, which is a bunch of guys going through a really fucking ridiculously self-indulgent period of trying to get the band back together as a result of being successful."

Lead single 'You Could Be Mine' was indicative of Guns' still blazing passion for straight-up hard rock, though it was misleading as to the remaining material on the album. To their credit, Guns were liberal with song-writing honours. Duff popped up with some credits, but mostly *Use Your Illusion* was down to Slash, Axl and Izzy. Given the three opposing styles of the composers, it was no surprise *Use Your Illusion* was so diverse but by comparing the credits and songs from each writer, it's easy to distinguish the different styles.

As G N' R started to increase in notoriety, their record sales followed. Predictably there was to be a lot of in-fighting as particular people in the band felt they were not getting their due. As chief peacemaker, Slash took the responsibility "of figuring out who wrote what parts of a song or part of a song," according to Axl. "There were four categories, I believe. There were lyrics, melody, music – meaning guitars, bass and drums – and accompaniment and arrangement. And we split each one of those into twenty five percent."

Given that between 1988 and 1992, the band were rumoured to have generated an income in the region of $60 million, it is easy to see why the percentage splits were important. This kind of income was distinctly rare for a new band – the likes of Paul McCartney and David Bowie might enjoy regular earnings in the tens of millions, but only after a sustained career and a back catalogue featuring scores of albums. G N' R were *massive*.

"*Use Your Illusion* is the result of conquering what Kurt Cobain couldn't," Slash would say. All Slash had ever wanted was to be a guitar player but for *Use Your Illusion,* he was more of an all-rounder. He had to keep relations with Axl productive and bouyant, work seamlessly with Izzy, and make a wealth of extra musicians, from his new drummer to the multitude of backing singers, feel welcome. Though many would feel it was all about Axl, Slash also deserves much credit for his role in harvesting the *Use Your Illusion* experience.

The first time Slash popped up with a writing credit was on the languid 'Dust N' Bones'. The main singing parts were handled by Stradlin and the bulk of the music was composed by the two guitarists.

It was one of the band's finer moments, showcasing Izzy's lead vocal abilities and song-writing prowess. It's one of the few songs on the *Use Your Illusion* albums to not feature an Axl Rose credit and the lazy, stroking rock 'n' roll proves Stradlin's desire to mellow out musically (his later solo albums would also bear this out, such as the underrated *117°* opus). The lyrics were a veritable shrug of the shoulders to the pressures of life, especially while in a famous rock band. Stradlin seemed to be indignant at the melee often surrounding him.

The words echoed Slash's attitude – a carefree lament for times past. But despite the low-slung swagger of the sentiments, the song featured a fine set of lead guitar from Slash as the song is brought humming to life. For such a bog standard blues take, 'Dust N' Bones' is a very entertaining track and one of the underrated gems on the *Use Your Illusion* albums.

'Perfect Crime' was the next song with a Slash credit and was far more brutal in its vocal assault. Axl is in fine form as a pent-up singer, mixing a complicated series of notes and skits into the space of just over two minutes. The track proved both Slash and Izzy could come up with fiery guitar parts when needed and 'Perfect

Crime' was the perfect foil coming in between 'Don't Cry (Original)' and the tongue-in-cheek 'You Ain't The First'. The former was a terrific 'power ballad', a long standing Guns tune that was finally immortalised in two different versions, featuring alternate lyrics.

"One thing about this album," Slash said, "is that a lot of these songs were written during different time periods for us – some of them even before we met one another. So what happens is, you have lyrics to a song and some music that one of the other guys wrote a long time ago, and you go in to record it, and you can't catch the vibe he had at whatever time he wrote it". 'Don't Cry' was a perfect example. The song first appeared on G N' R's first demo tape in 1986. It was also a firm live favourite causing a different kind of ripple in the crowd as the band laid its emotions bare to offset the snarling menace of tracks such as 'Welcome To The Jungle'. In the end were three versions of 'Don't Cry' – the original demo, the finished version, and an adaptation featuring alternate lyrics.

The solo from Slash is partly what made 'Don't Cry' a classic G N' R moment. 'Perfect Crime' also featured some standout guitar playing, especially in the background to the bridge section. Axl spits his confrontational lyrics while Slash fingers the guitar neck speedily and bouyantly. And after the hi-octane burst of "1,2,3,4,5,6,7,8" Slash is on fire, blasting radiant notes from his axe whilst constantly holding the hub of the song together. With another roll up the frets, the song is over in a flash, leaving the listener craving more.

The heaviest song on the whole of *Use Your Illusion* was the next one with a Slash credit, 'Garden Of Eden'. This time it was down to just him and Axl – a pounding full-on velocity number (featuring an equally vivid and frantic video with Axl taking supreme close up, centre stage). Again there is some superb subliminal guitar taking backstage behind Axl's increasingly incredible rants. This frantic offsetting of guitar and vocals certainly worked well and the track begged for other similar material which is somewhat lacking throughout the remainder of *Use Your Illusion* I & II. The lyrics are as lengthy as anything on the albums, yet are somehow squeezed into two and a half minutes, such is the speedy diatribe at play in the song. It was something of a curveball for the band, but all the more vital because of it.

Yet even when Slash did not receive an actual credit, he managed to steal the show, particularly on 'Don't Damn Me' which started with his trademark rhythmic swagger and turned out to be one of the highlights of the first *Use Your Illusion* record.

Of course, the song only worked because of the bounding nature of the musical backing and Slash was the chief whip of the catchy notes pushing the song along. Dave Lank also popped up with his one and only credit but the music was pure Slash. There was the breakdown section with a typical Slash solo, winding and bending the mid-range notes whilst mimicking Axl's delivery, before bringing the song back to full speed with the intro riff once again. The ending refrain of the track also brings this riff screaming to life in a higher key as the song builds to a crescendo. Again this was one of the standout tracks of the whole set.

Next up for Slash was a joint effort with Duff, Izzy and Axl but the song 'Bad Apples' was a fairly horrible funk/blues affair, which had been leaked onto a radio show before *Use Your Illusion* was released. Sure, on another album – especially by a different band – this would have been a catchy and acceptable track but in amongst the musical riches of *Use Your Illusion* it was predictable and sub-standard, hell, there weren't even any guitar highlights! There was a fairly extended solo from Slash which carried the song to a degree, yet somehow it all seemed out of place and one of the biggest departures for the Guns N' Roses of old.

This track also seems to pale in comparison to the closing track on the first *Use Your Illusion* album, the emotional 'Coma'. "I wrote some really cool shit when I was high," Slash would grin. "I wrote that loaded. And it's not something that I can really see myself writing right now."

The song was definitely heavy, lyrically, emotionally and musically. "I like it a lot," Slash would gush. "It's got a defibrillator in it you know, the instrument that starts your heart when it's stopped. And there's some EKG beeps too. We were just fucking around, but the song is heavy, and Axl's vocals are gorgeous, I mean really amazing."

Though the epic 'November Rain' would take chief plaudits on the album, 'Coma' was a very worthy contender for best song of *Use Your Illusion I*. Combining everything Guns had become famous for – squealing, heartfelt vocals, a merger of emotional and heavy guitar parts and the requisite series of break-down sections, this track had a particularly weighty intermission – literally mimicking a succession of real doctors trying to save someone's life.

"Writing 'Coma' was so heavy I'd start to write and

I'd just pass out. I tried to write that song for a year... I wrote the whole end of that song off the top of my head. It just poured out," Axl would say. It is certainly one of the most ambitious tracks the band had so far recorded, ten minutes and thirteen seconds of intense emotional trauma. Though the song was linked by some to an alleged drugs overdose, the far more likely explanation would be it is a depiction of an 'emotional' coma. During the song Axl has to be 'zapped' back to life by doctors, whilst in his mind a myriad of female voices reprimanding him are spoken incessantly. The women are referred to in the liner notes as 'bitches' and named, along with the genuine doctor who also contributes a sound bite, Dr. Michael Smolens.

In the notes, Axl would thank Slash for his emotive guitar playing on 'Coma'. It is no wonder given the heart-wrenching, soulful glide, which truly takes the song to another level. There were few guitarists alive who could match such a poignant series of notes. Slash also beautifully combines with Axl for the ending rant – wringing his guitar to collide with each changing key in the frontman's voice.

'November Rain' may not have featured a writing credit for Slash – Rose was credited as the sole composer – but, as guitar magazines around the world would often say – the main solo in the song was one of the best of all-time. The song truly showed by how much – and to where – Guns had progressed. Despite the old favourite, 'Sweet Child O' Mine' G N' R had never in the past attempted such an ambitious love torn melody. Come 1991, they were finally able to match their ambitions with an appropriate budget which meant 'November Rain' included piano, a keyboard orchestra and expensive synthesizers. The result was a mammoth track, pulsed with Axl's heart stirring lyrics and melodies.

Slash's guitar truly set the song off, from the backing to the words leading up to the first guitar solo which then ebbed and flowed like a true soft metal anthem, bubbling with trademark Slash bends. It was not merely doing his duty to come up with a suitable solo, he was transcending the expected and making the song come alive. Anyone could lay down an appropriate section of the right notes but few could have brought such soul to the same ideas.

Axl Rose felt this was the song he had always wanted to write and finally accomplished that ambition. As the song edges towards its climax, Slash again launches into a blinding solo, bringing 'November Rain' to soaring new heights and creating an enduring memory for every listener. For the promotional video, he equally laid down a lasting visual, playing alone near the church (which was the scene for the 'wedding' between Axl and then-girlfriend Stephanie Seymour) with hair tousled by the wind and his Les Paul sauntering high above his head.

For *Use Your Illusion II,* Slash's credits were more sparse, with writing contributions to three songs: 'Civil War', 'Get In The Ring' and 'Locomotive'. It is arguable that this trio was among the strongest tracks on the entire record and with the exception of 'You Could Be Mine', 'Estranged' and 'Knockin' On Heaven's Door' certainly the most memorable of the set. The latter, a Bob Dylan cover, was brought kicking into the 1990s with a high quality production and some superb, yet neatly simple acoustic guitar playing from Slash.

Guns' own material was even stronger. Opener 'Civil War' showed that here was a band progressing at an alarming pace, it almost did not sound like the Guns N' Roses of old in some places. Axl's adaptable voice was so unpredictable, it was only when he lurched into a deep scream that one associated the music with Axl and G N' R. Piano littered the first track, the only song where Steven Adler received a playing credit. It had been the first song completed for the *Use Your Illusion* sessions and it was one of the best. It was perhaps more epic than any other track, and certainly unique in its criticism of war.

'Get In The Ring' showcased the other side of the band – the snotty, brash, arrogant and confrontational side. It was one of the reasons we loved Guns N' Roses. Essentially a diatribe against the continually critical music press and the lies they often 'revealed' about the group, it broke down into a verbal tirade unbeaten before or since by any big standing rock act.

Guns were not frightened to personally name-check individuals who had overstepped the mark in trying to make good copy. As the band would later explain in interviews, kids who loved the group would spend what little money they had in order to read about their favourite band only for the shit they read to be incorrect or exaggerated. So there was short shrift for the likes of *Kerrang!, Spin* and *Hit Parader* who all were named along with their appropriate contributor who had written about the band over in some way. Yes, it was bravado when Axl invited all of the detractors into the 'ring' and perhaps ill-advised to do so, but it was a very human aspect of the band and their listeners lapped it up. Loveable, controversial and somewhat juvenile but, oh so brilliant.

Which made the likes of drawn out epics such as

'Estranged', 'Breakdown' and the Slash co-penned 'Locomotive' all the more special. The latter was the most complicated song on the *Use Your Illusion* albums, intertwining a succession of seemingly opposing riffs, melodies and ideas into one huge overwrought power ballad. It was a trademark rant from Axl, lamenting the intricacies and downsides to being in love. Though the track was brought to varying heights with the Slash solo spots, it was frequently slammed back down to earth by the increasingly longer Axl rallies. It was more like an extended jam session than a cohesive song but still, it commands a strong place in the *Use Your Illusion* pantheon and again marked out an increasing circle of G N' R capabilities.

★ ★ ★

Perhaps bizarrely, although the *Use Your Illusion* albums would propel Guns N' Roses to immense global success, the project did not sit well with Slash and he would distance himself from the compliments over the double set. "*Use Your Illusion* sounded amazing when it was just the basic tracks," he would surprisingly say. "It was fucking great. But then by the time all the tracks were done it was like impossible to fucking mix it, and it came out sounding...The more stuff you put on tape, the less 'big' it sounds ... But I'm not gonna do it that way again, and that's what we have to talk about."

It is easy to see with hindsight that Guns could not carry on as they were. You have to agree with Slash in at least one way. There were a series of added effects on the *Use Your Illusion* material, many of which were, in the author's opinion, unnecessary – a great song is great regardless of the additional production or extra instruments. So many musicians make the mistake of adding parts simply because they can. Yet they fail to see the classic bands and the most memorable songs, are usually the simplest. Even Guns' own idols such as the Rolling Stones and Aerosmith were hardly known for rampant experimentation with sounds or a harem of extra musos onstage – they just wrote great songs.

Slash was entirely justified in pointing this out to Axl and he was perhaps the closest to the frontman and able to suggest such a thing. Perhaps one day the world will hear the alternative *Use Your Illusion* – before the material was expanded. Slash revealed to www.gnrsource.com that he has "the rough mixes, which are more or less the basic tracks and the basic overdubs – very simplified – and those fucking rock! I could play you *Use Your Illusion* before it went into the mixing stage, and you'd be like, 'Fucking what?!' It's very brash. But this is before synthesizers and all this outside stuff got involved."

"I really try to understand where Axl's coming from when he gets into that," he continued. "It's a self-expression that, because our personalities are so different, I can't fucking understand. And he probably can't understand why I want to keep everything so natural. But it's just because I know the band – on a players' level or an emotional level or an expression level – is fine when it's naked on its own. When we play live, it's right there, y'know? That's as good as you're gonna be, no matter what you put on it."

It is, of course, all subjective and Axl would argue (probaby rightly) that the massive sales and critical acclaim vindicated his creative experimentation. That said, how many people who own the *Use Your Illusion* records love them for the production or instruments rather than the songs themselves. It is the songs that remain. In 2003, when The Beatles released *Let It Be Naked,* the response was overwhelming and many felt the reworked version was superior to the original. The 1970 classic was undisputedly a superb album yet it is very interesting to hear the record as Paul McCartney reputedly intended. There were quite brilliant orchestral embellishments on the original, yet as millions would concur, hearing the stripped down versions simply seemed to give the songs a greater weight. The less at play musically the more emotional a song can be and it would not lose its impact either.

Slash feels that, "With *Use Your Illusion*, we were going through so much of a mish-mash of all kinds, personal changes and this, that and the other. The fact that we completed those albums is unbelievable. You might be able to go to a store and buy it and listen to it, but you'll never be able to understand the emotional turmoil that was going on from adjusting from being some piece of shit club band to all of a sudden being like, quote, 'The biggest band in the world' and having that attention thrown at you, and having the pressures that go along with it and all this ridiculous stuff."

Slash was not merely referring to the albums but rather the ensuing tour which would really take G N' R over the edge. For those in the band who felt the recording sessions were overblown and unnecessary, they were about to see that touring in the biggest band in the world was no breeze either.

Chapter 9

THE DOWNWARD SPIRAL

**"I LOVE BEING IN THE STUDIO. RECORDING THE ALBUMS
WASN'T HARD; IT WAS RECOVERING FROM MAJOR DRUG PROBLEMS.
AXL'S NEVER BEEN ADDICTEDTO ANYTHING – EXCEPT MAYBE
CIGARETTES. I'VE NEVER BEEN STRUNGOUT ON TOUR EVER."**
SLASH

Albums as expansive as *Use Your Illusion I & II* were always going to be difficult to recreate live. Yet instead of doing what most bands would do and improvising or leaving out certain additional instruments, Axl Rose was not about to be left wanting onstage. Between him and Guns' management there were several backing singers hired for all the *Use Your Illusion* dates as well as copious additional musicians. Literally, this was not just Guns N' Roses anymore. Slash was becoming tired of what the band had become. That said, the fans didn't seem to mind, despite occasional gig 'problems'. The 'Use Your Illusion' tour was one of the biggest and most successful jaunts by a rock band *ever*.

Behind the scenes, however, tension was rife and

events remained complex. When G N' R played at the Riverport Amphitheatre in Maryland Heights, a riot was caused by the leader of a local biker gang, who'd been harassing fans in the front row. Axl asked for the security men to throw him out, but they were apparently friends of the biker gang and they ignored the understandably vexed frontman. The biker proceeded to goad the Guns' frontman by waving a camera. Axl again asked the security to extradite the biker. Once more they ignored his pleas. After several fans managed to get to Axl and grab both his ankles and two bottles were thrown at Duff, Axl took matters into his own hands; during 'Rocket Queen' he jumped into the crowd to confront the biker.

"Thanks to the lame ass security, I'm going home!" Axl announced when he returned to the stage. However the band did initially intend to come back to finish their set, as long as Axl could locate a contact lens, after one had been lost during his encounter. "I went backstage and found a new lens. It was getting crazy, and we decided we were going to go back out and try to play, because we didn't want people to get hurt..." Axl said. But before Axl and the band could return, the crowd had destroyed the drum set. There was a resultant riot, which led to damage in several areas, not least of which were breakages to equipment that caused another three shows to be cancelled. "We were backstage, watching cops on stretchers all bloody and shit, and it was like, 'Fuck! How could this be happening?'" recalled a contemplative Slash in *RIP*. "I was so scared somebody was going to die. It was completely out of hand. The kids had a field day. I lost all my amps, my guitar tech got a bottle in the head, someone got knifed, our stage and video equipment and Axl's piano were trashed. It shouldn't have happened... but it did."

Sixty fans were injured and sixteen were arrested. Around $200,000 worth of damage was caused. Legal letters flew. Slash tried to put the farcical event into perspective. "I feel bad for what happened, but I can't just say it was our fault. And I won't blame the kids of St. Louis, either. It just happened. I'm not putting the rap on anybody." After the St. Louis incident, the band received a lot of flak and from then on many promoters were nervous about endorsing a Guns N' Roses gig. A concert due to take place at Lake Compounce Amphitheatre in Bristol, Connecticut was cancelled because the residents living near the venue were afraid of a riot breaking out. Events were escalating by the day.

It was actually behind the scenes where problems

were really beginning to bubble, however. After Adler's departure, things had not been quite the same between the remaining band members. Izzy was frequently at odds with Axl and, surprisingly perhaps, remained pretty unmoved by the Guns' high profile. Izzy was not overly excited by super-stardom and was nonchalant about playing in large venues. A show that the band played at Wembley Stadium in London, England on August 31, 1991, was to be Stradlin's last.

The band necessarily began to look for a touring guitarist. After considering Dave Navarro, once of Jane's Addiction (later the Red Hot Chili Peppers and a solo artist), the band found a suitable candidate in Gilby Clarke, who had been in Kill For Thrills. He was an acquaintance of the band, having plied his trade around Hollywood for the best part of a decade.

Once he had established himself as a Guns member, Axl and Slash also joined him on his first solo album, *Pawnshop Guitars*. "Gilby is awesome, and a pleasure to be around" Axl gushed. "He works the stage and the crowd really well. He has his opinions of what's going on with us, and it helps us get a different perspective. He's been putting himself through his own rock and roll education with his other groups for years. Now he's a part of Guns N' Roses."

Fans accepted the six-stringer unequivocally. Not only did Gilby look very similar to Izzy, but also his guitar style underlined the Guns' songs with a strikingly similar languid technique. Gilby performed his first show with the band at the Worcester Centrum Centre in Worcester, MA on December 5, 1991. Towards the end of the month the video for 'November Rain' was filmed providing the band with a visual peak that would ensure the name Guns N' Roses remained memorable long after their sell-by date.

In May of 1992, Slash joined Metallica's Lar Ulrich at a press conference to announce a duel headlining tour of Guns N' Roses and Metallica for the summer in the United States. This was, without doubt, one of the biggest tours of all-time in the world of heavy metal. Despite the obvious difference between the two bands' styles, and their fans to some degree, they were the two biggest acts in the world of rock and to see them link up together in such an unprecedented event thrilled fans. Lars Ulrich was, by his own admission, the one "closest to some of those guys" and spoke of "late night drinking babbles where we would speak about actually going out and playing some gigs together."

Slash commented, "I just like to play guitar. It wasn't

about business, or trying to be cool on Sunset Strip, or getting the cover of fuckin' *Rolling Stone*, or any of that. It was about just getting together with a bunch of guys that could cause something. Even if we weren't all on the exact same page as far as direction goes, somehow we managed to make a band that was a mixture of everything – of attitude. At the time, the five of us were the only people who could have made up Guns N' Roses and that I'm proud of." It is the perspective of a guitarist who simply wanted to do his job, however remarkable that job happened to be, and remain away from the hustle and bustle of touring life – which was at odds with the off-stage antics of G N' R at the time. In one notable side issue, G N' R were the subject of a complaint by 57,000 Metallica fans after the concert in Montreal, Canada. It was business as usual.

The band was now *so* big and *so* famous, that fact and fiction seemed to blur at times. Slash made reference to this surreality when speaking to *Kerrang!* "The older you get and the more you do this, the more significant the *Spinal Tap* movie becomes. The funny thing about it is, it's so fucking accurate! There was one time during the stadium tour with Guns N' Roses where we had the worst show I think we ever had. We were in the dressing room before we went on, watching that whole movie, before Axl was ready to go on stage. Then we went out there, and I'll tell you that I would never watch *Spinal Tap* before a show again ... ever!"

1992 threatened to be Guns N' Roses most shambolic year – yet perversely massive in commercial terms. After the highs of finally releasing the *Use Your Illusion* double set and beginning to tour in support of it, there was an imminent danger of the core of the band being disrupted. As Axl made reference to that year, the band was, in many ways, run by him and Slash. However, against some people's expectations, Axl relished the grand scale and was happy to credit those he felt were contributing. He went on to say, "Guns N' Roses is basically Slash, Duff, Doug Goldstein and myself, but there's a lot of other people involved that are a part of our lives and a part of our family. I love everybody in this band. It's kicking ass and feels really warm and really cool onstage. At this point it's the twelve of us that get onstage and fucking go all out. There's Teddy, there's Dizzy, there's Roberta, Tracy, Lisa, CeCe, Anne, Gilby, Matt, Duff, Slash and me. Slash put this new band together, did all of the groundwork. He did such an amazing job that I just can't believe it really happened. I'm glad to be a part of it."

When Guns were hired to tour with the Rolling Stones, it impacted on them heavily. Although Axl had always been at the centre of everything, seeing Stones' frontman Mick Jagger's ruthless business streak and attention to detail set him on his own personal crusade. While he made comments that Slash should take note of regarding the Stones' work ethic ("after working with Jagger it was like, don't anybody ever call me a dictator again! You go work for the Stones and you'll find out the hard way what working for a real dictator is like!") he subsequently became a very meticulous operator. Axl seemed to admire the fact that Jagger walked off stage and immersed himself in paper work.

He stated that Jagger was "involved in every little aspect of the show, from what the backing singers are getting paid to what a particular part of the PA costs to buy or hire. He is on top of all of it." Though Axl claimed that he "doesn't sit around checking the gate receipts at the end of every show," he did concede that somebody had to take the responsibility of frontman and that, "the guitar player can't do it because he is not the guy who has to be communicating directly with

Right: Slash (3rd row, 2nd from left), then a relatively new kid in Los Angeles, poses for his 6th grade class photo in 1977.

Left: Slash plays with his band during a lunch break at Fairfax High School, Los Angeles in 1982. The school counts fellow rock legends Anthony Kiedis and Flea among its alumni as well as Slash and Tracii Guns.

Right: Slash with his already impressive collection of guitars in his bedroom in 1983.

Above: Duff McKagan, Izzy Stradlin, Axl Rose, Steven Adler and Slash, the most famous Guns N' Roses line-up, in June 1985. © *Jack Lue/Michael Ochs Archives/Getty Images*

Below: The iconic duo of Axl Rose and Slash performing at the Troubadour in Los Angeles on 28 February 1986. Tom Zutaut of Geffen Records was in attendance, and would later sign them to a record deal with the label.

© *Marc S Canter/Michael Ochs Archives/Getty Images*

Above: Two rock legends together: Brian May and Slash at the Freddie Mercury Tribute Concert at Wembley Stadium on 20 April 1992.   © *Michael Putland/Getty Images*

Below: Performing as part of Slash's Snakepit at the Monsters of Rock festival at Donington Park in August 1995.   © *Mick Hutson/Redferns/Getty Images*

Above: Slash and Ronnie Wood pose during Woods's gallery opening in 2002 in Beverly Hills.
© David Klein/Getty Images

Below left: Slash and Perla pictured together in 2004.
© Chris Polk/FilmMagic

Below right: On stage with Duff McKagan, now as part of supergroup Velvet Revolver, at Lowlands Festival in the Netherlands in 2004.
© Paul Bergen/Redferns

the audience with eye-contact and body movements. He can go back, hang his hair down in his face and stand by the amps and just get into his guitar part." Although this assessment of a frontman's role is fair, many read this quote from www.snakepit.org as a not so veiled dig at Slash.

Later, the Stones would provide Slash with some help. "Mick and Keith were really instrumental in keeping my head together about the lead singer/lead guitar player relationship," he said. "I was watching them from the sidelines as they were working in the studio, and we're not the only ones that go through it, y'know?"

After a reported advance from Geffen of $10 million, Guns N' Roses were supposed to begin the recording for the follow up to the *Use Your Illusion* albums; yet, they tinkered with cover versions which should have been released years earlier. *The Spaghetti Incident?* met with confusion amongst many fans and was to be a commercial downslide for G N' R. Though it sold relatively well, especially for a covers album – it was nevertheless dwarfed by sales of the bands previous work.

"They were recording at A&M across the street from Crazy Horse on LaBrea, now Crazy Girls," says an old acquaintance of the band. "It is a strip joint and I was dancing there and Matt and Slash came in every day to play pool. They were such fun people, Duff may have come in as well but I was closest with Slash. They were very friendly, respectable and good tippers. Slash and me would sit across from each other and discuss relationships, I don't remember much but he was quite erotic. On the last day of their recording, as they were saying goodbye to us all, I wanted to make a last impression and put on this perfume, much too much. And when I walked up to Slash he said to me, 'Wwwoooooooo man, you stink!' It was my turn on stage and the very last I ever saw of Slash is that I was on all fours with my butt in the air and he put five dollars in my t-back/g-string. Bye Slash, it was fun, happy to play pool and talk sex with you any day. And I did stink, you were right..."

The idea was for each member to pick their favourite songs and the band to attack them in their own style. In much the same way as *G N' R Lies*, the covers album was really intended as a stop-gap before the next 'real' album. Covering the dirty underside of music was a brave move at the time and the actual year was not the best one in which to release such a set. Many of Guns' fans were too young to remember the originals and as such were rather perplexed or disappointed at the 'old school' feel of the album. Although in the liner notes the band advised, "a great song can be found anywhere. Do yourself a favour and go find the originals," it seemed there were not many who were interested.

It was a great shame. *The Spaghetti Incident?* became something of a neglected release in the G N' R back catalogue. Whether it was the cryptic title, the staid artwork (literally a photo of tinned spaghetti) or the choice of relatively obscure songs, the album became the band's worst selling. Yet, in some senses, perhaps they appreciated the lukewarm reception. After Izzy had departed, it was ironic that the band essentially revisited their roots and stripped everything down. They forgot about orchestras and copious female backing singers, instead concentrating on guitar, bass, drums and Axl's highly flexible voice.

"I wanted to do 'Hair of the Dog', T-Rex's 'Buick Makane', and Fear's 'I Don't Care About You'," he told www.metaverse.com. "Those are songs that meant much to me," Slash explained of his choices. "Axl always hums on 'Since I Don't Have You', and he loves 'Black Leather' so those were his choices. Duff picked 'Down On The Farm', and we all wanted to do a song by the New York Dolls. It became 'Human Being'."

The true theme of the album seemed to be a mixture of fun and anger. Songs such as the rowdy 'I Don't Care About You' epitomised Guns' idiom. A predominantly 'punk' tribute album wouldn't have been complete without a Sex Pistols track, but the band chose a strangely sultry number in 'Black Leather'. "I met Steve Jones from the Sex Pistols at [a] wedding," Slash said. "He asked when the record came out and if our version of 'Black Leather' sounded better then the 'cover' the Runaways did. 'Absolutely, I said, it sounds better than your version too ...'"

The relaxed sounding album came from the stress free vibe the band enjoyed whilst recording. Gilby was a peaceful guitar player who always hit the right notes but didn't throw tantrums or question others' parts. As Slash remarked with a smile, "I love recording like this. During *Appetite For Destruction*, *G N' R Lies* and *Use Your Illusion* I had to put up with Izzy the whole time! I never liked playing with him. It was wonderful to escape on this record. It sounds tighter and so much cooler than anything we've done before."

★　★　★

1993 was a year for change in the music industry, especially the rock and alternative scenes. Nirvana had virtually single-handedly transformed the entire business with their *Nevermind* album (ironically released on the Geffen label). Almost overnight the desire for good time hard rock music vanished as the so-called 'grunge' genre found success in lyrics more concerned with the harsh reality of everyday life. The 'loser' culture was everywhere and soon 'thrift store' chic would find its way on to the catwalk, where jackets costing $3000 would ape the $25 coat Cobain originally wore. By then, the genre had been stripped of all its original venom; for now, it was revolutionary. For some, Guns N' Roses looked dated overnight.

Though Guns N' Roses sat somewhere within the hard rock category, they were equally fortunate enough to have covered the gamut of emotions, not to mention instruments and styles, on their last two albums. Where lesser acts such as Poison and Warrant fell completely off the scale, Guns retained their credibility by virtue of the range of their material. This was due in part to their astonishing longevity in the press; they *always* sold magazines. Since severing all contact with the media (a decision somewhat explained on 'Get In The Ring'), Axl had created an aura of mystique around G N' R and people were still remarkably concerned with Guns' movements. Therefore the follow up to *Use Your Illusion 1 & 2* was hotly awaited, despite the seismic change in the musical landscape, post-*Nevermind*.

While the early 1990s undoubtedly belonged to grunge, there was soon to be a new punk movement. When it came (with The Offspring and Green Day releasing *Smash* and *Dookie* respectively) it effectively killed the last vestiges of the commercial rock and metal scene. Quite coincidentally, Guns had long been considering a punk revival, with a tribute album that was way overdue. The original plan was to precede *Use Your Illusion 1 & 2* with the covers opus, but instead the songs lay unused until the Guns N' Roses comeback was decided.

★ ★ ★

In the aftermath of *The Spaghetti Incident?*, the situation dramatically worsened. Gilby Clarke parted ways with the band – not a development they were all happy with – and legal letters flew once more. Further, the relationship between Axl and Slash began to disintegrate.

Behind the scenes things were going downhill fast for the Gunners. Some years before, Axl had set the ball rolling to exclusively own the Guns N' Roses name. In hindsight, Slash and Duff were very upset at themselves for being so naïve. Slash said, "I was blindsided by it, more or less a legal faux pas. I'd be lying to say I wasn't a little bit peeved at that – he can actually go and record a Guns N' Roses album without the consent of the other members of the band."

One of the reasons behind the souring relationship between Slash and Axl was the fact that one of the guitarist's ex-girlfriends testified against Axl in a court appearance, about allegations of physical abuse. Another lawsuit against Axl by a woman was also the focus of much media attention at this time too ... the lawyers were very busy. The cases brought against Axl were eventually settled. Nonetheless, the increasing complexity of all things 'Axl' did little to calm the turbulent waters.

Eventually, the relationship between Slash and Axl would crumble terminally. When it came, the end of them both as a partnership was effectively the end of the old Guns N' Roses. Work for the double live album *Live Era '87-'93* was handled by Axl and the ex-members separately, with Axl and Slash only communicating via their respective managers, Doug Goldstein and Tom Maher. While Duff and Slash happily worked together, Axl would be sent CDs and worked alternate shifts to the other members in the studio. It was the final admonishment for the old line-up.

The Spaghetti Incident? preceded the end for all the remaining G N' R members bar Axl Rose. Subsequent to the covers album, Guns went on to record one song, a cover of the Rolling Stones' 'Sympathy For The Devil' for the Tom Cruise movie *Interview With The Vampire.* Though it was passable as a new track there was somehow something lacking from the song. It certainly seemed as if the band was not quite together ... and so it proved.

"Granted it sort of sounds like Guns N' Roses, but it was my vehicle to help get the band into one room," Slash would admit. "But who shows up? It's Duff and Matt and me who do the whole track, then Axl did the other bit by himself a week later. That wasn't my idea of something that we should've released, and it definitely wasn't what I was hoping for to be the thread that was going to get the band back together."

It seemed ironic that Slash, Izzy and Duff wanted to go back to basics, yet in doing so and recording a raw punk covers record, they alienated many of the fans who had hopped on the Guns' bandwagon after the *Use Your Illusion* set. Perhaps Axl was doing something right after all. The frontman had not been averse to doing a covers album and he agreed with everyone having their own choice of songs, but deep down he was itching to create a modern, epic masterpiece and pick up where *Use Your Illusion* left off.

Slash and the other musicians who were left from the *Appetite For Destruction* days simply preferred things uncomplicated, from the style of the music to the type of tours they wanted to undertake. First Duff released a solo album, *Believe In Me* in 1993. In 1997, Izzy Stradlin would release his first solo record, under the name Izzy Stradlin & The Ju-Ju Hounds.

"We accomplished *Use Your Illusion* and then we took off on this world-wide fucking mega-rock star thing," Slash recalled in *RIP* about the G N' R circus. "So then we come home, and there's like the accountants and all these people, all these people who are part of the business, telling you to invest your money – 'You have to buy a house'. I bought a house. I went through the closest thing to what you'd call suicidal depression after I'd laid in my bed in my house by myself, staring at the ceiling for days on end, not knowing what the fuck to do with myself. I couldn't hang out on the street like I normally did, because everybody looked at me differently, treated me differently, and I didn't like it. It was really hard."

Slash was not alone. Most touring musicians were ill-equipped for the surreal experience of trying to adjust to home life after years on the road, but those close to Slash, such as Duff and Izzy, were going through the same difficulties. Duff especially was trying hard to keep fit and stay substance free whilst simultaneously aimng to keep Guns N' Roses together. Everyone expected a new album to come relatively soon after *The Spaghetti Incident?* but no one knew, not even Axl, that it would be at least fifteen years before a full new studio record would ever emerge. After underlining the conflict in touring choices (Slash wanted to play small clubs in support of *The Spaghetti Incident?*, Axl did not) the laid-back guitarist considered the future of the band and specifically his relationship with Rose within the ranks. "I don't [know] where Axl's head's at," he mused. "I really need to sit down and talk to the guy about how we're fucking gonna find some common ground here. I don't mind going back and playing the odd stadium, but I would like to keep us more of an indoor kind of thing. We need to figure out how to establish more of a common ground with the kids that we're playing for, because I feel the same now as I did way back when, where you just go out and hang out with 'em and you feel so comfortable. This 'above ground' kind of rock star status that say, Bon Jovi enjoys, I don't really get into it. But I'm not depressed or pessimistic about the whole thing; I feel very optimistic, I'm just not sure what's gonna happen. I just wanna be able to go and do it and know that the spark is there, because when the spark's there it just flows."

Inevitably, Slash's mind began to wander and ideas for his own project began to gestate – Slash's Snakepit was thus conceived. Slash felt that he needed to exercise his creative muscle while Guns simmered and initially he didn't want this new project to be a full-time concern, it was merely to continue the low key vibe he preferred, write some good rock 'n' roll tunes and go back to playing small venues once more.

"I'm writing material that's just the same as the kind of material I used to write in the old days," the six stringer said of his ideas. "Everybody used to go, 'What's gonna happen [to Guns] when a new fad comes along?' or whatever. And I'd be, 'I don't give a fuck!' And I watched [grunge] happen, and it didn't matter to me. With Axl it mattered a hell of a lot."

Slash was referring to the inexplicable hype surrounding Seattle grungers like Pearl Jam and how that particular band had quickly found themselves not just the darlings of the independent music press but worldwide rock stars, belying their humble roots. Axl admired this messiah status whilst Slash just wanted to sneak off and hide somewhere. It was a conflict that was bound to cause ructions and eventually led to the demise of a beautiful partnership.

"We do what we do the best that anybody does," he told *Kerrang!* "Let's just go out and do a club tour, a theatre tour, and fucking get back down to where we have some validity with an audience that we can relate to," Slash continued. "But Axl was all fucking…he wants to be on MTV, he wants to do *Unplugged* … so we didn't see eye to eye, and that's where a lot of that bullshit got started, and of course it was blown out of all proportion in the press."

It was perhaps almost inevitable that Axl would struggle with the new material that Slash put forward for Guns N' Roses. He knew Slash wanted to keep things as basic as possible, of course there would be guitar solos and bouyant riffs but no air of pretensions – no row of backing singers, no brass sections or twenty-five minute piano solos. "I played him the material that I was writing, and he was like, 'I don't wanna do that kind of music,' Slash deadpanned. "The stuff that he was into, I couldn't understand." The issue of who 'owned' the name Guns N' Roses was central to the new material being created by respective members.

With Axl seemingly on a never-ending quest for stadium rock god status, Slash had to get his rocks off elsewhere. "I went back to work," he explained matter-of-factly to www.gnrsource.com. "I built a studio in my house, I kept myself busy. I had the first multi-track studio I've ever had, so I was like a kid in a candy store, and I started playing and recorded all this stuff.

To get back to a place where I feel like I'm still struggling is the greatest feeling. I don't think I would have made it had I not done that. I think my situation would be worse – having to deal with Axl and Guns N' Roses – had I just hung around and waited. [Working on his own material] has been a real shot in the arm. "I mean, that's what rock 'n' roll [is] to me . You don't have to be a musician to have what I consider to be a rock 'n' roll attitude; it's a way of doing things. To be on stage, that was it. The rest of it was just some sort of fantastical nightmare."

When the Guns N' Roses tour finally ground to a

halt after nearly thirty months of being on the road, Slash was, ironically, as rejuvenated as ever. With the concept of his fledgling project – the Snakepit – still forming, he genuinely felt the sky was the limit.

Chapter 10

ENTER THE SNAKE

**"AXL WAS ON A DIFFERENT TRIP, WHERE HE WANTED TO
SOUND LIKE PEARL JAM, LAST I HEARD, WITH KEYBOARDS,
AND HEAVY-DUTY EPIC VIDEOS. THAT WAS ALL REALLY
TEDIOUS FOR ME, THIS KEPT ME SANE."**
SLASH

Slash's back to basics ethic would herald the recording of a very special album. Featuring Guns' members Matt Sorum, Dizzy Reed, (*Use Your Illusion* harmonica player) Teddy Andreadis and ex-axe slinger Gilby Clarke, the nucleus of the band also included bass player Mike Inez of Alice In Chains and a curveball in the form of ex-Jellyfish guitarist Eric Dover. For Slash's new project, Dover would handle lead vocals at the suggestion of Gilby Clarke's drummer Mark Danziesen, which was to prove an insightful decision. He joined the five piece for an album which would be called *It's 5 O' Clock Somewhere*. The monicker for the outfit would be Slash's Snakepit at the insistence of Geffen who weren't too enthused at Slash's simple suggestion of Snakepit. They knew adding his name would boost sales.

With typical humility, Slash would say, "Snakepit is not supposed to be that big a deal. To verbally express how I feel about what I'm doing and the situation that's developed in Guns N' Roses is really hard for me."

Slash stood back from the obvious attention his side project was warranting, intriguingly claiming he didn't have any influences post-1979. But, whether intentional or otherwise, Snakepit did know what they were doing and the formula was simple. "The band is still a hard rock band," said Slash by way of explanation. "The music is the kind of stuff that I've always played and always want to do." They wrote fifty songs and whittled these down to the dozen they would record for the album. Slash enthused about how fresh the writing process had felt. "Everybody meshes really well and the chemistry is great. We all get along. Everybody is humble and appreciates everyone else's input."

The last comment was tell tale and though Slash would never be too hard on his former vocalist, many observers felt this was a clear reference to Axl Rose. Maybe there was no connection but it seemed that the more laid-back and approachable a muso was, the more instant their creations were. One only has to visit the solo work of Gilby Clarke – languid, almost dead-beat in its brand of skid row happy-go-lucky life. In Duff McKagan's solo work, we also see the same kind of balls-to-the-wall, plug in and play DIY ethics, something to be expected from someone of his background. And then there was Izzy with his brand of toe-tapping guitar – drugging the listener's brain with a somnambulant set of creepy yet catchy rock 'n' roll.

The interested observer could clearly see where the animosity lay in Guns N' Roses. Axl Rose would later speak of everyone's solo records as not being "suitable" for Guns and that therefore people could understand why he basically sought to run G N' R alone. Slash and Co. were unperturbed. They just wanted to get out and play, not spend over a decade perfecting one album. As far as Slash saw it, this rock thing was a simple affair and many fans respected those who just got out there and did it. No pretensions, no huge set-ups, just four or five guys with their basic instruments.

"The reality is, go buy those guys' solo records," Axl spat, referring to ex-members. "There are neat ideas and parts there, but they wouldn't have worked for a

Guns N' Roses records. There are people [out there] that I thought I was friends with who are all of a sudden in the magazines, going, 'They'll never get anywhere without Slash.' Thanks a lot. Like, I made this happen, you know. I basically figured out a way to save my own ass. There was only one way out, and I found it. Otherwise, you know, I believe my career was just going down the toilet. I figured out how to save my ass and then tried to bring everybody with me."

The new line-up of Guns N' Roses was coalescing around Axl nicely and he was certainly very focussed, as to be expected. "Along the time we were trying to put it together with the other fellas, I certainly had my doubts," G N' R manager Doug Goldstein remarked. "But now Axl has a [new] group of guys that he appears to be friends with, and it's a very cohesive unit, which wasn't necessarily the case in the past. Everything I've heard is spectacular. It's exciting and diverse and – I think – absolutely well worth the wait."

Axl spoke in interviews of how he was a little bemused by Slash's new approach and the variety of people he was playing with. This was perhaps ironic when you consider the sheer amount of 'special guests' Axl himself has roped in for Guns N' Roses since Slash departed. From basketball player Shaquille

O'Neal to ex-Pearl Jam drummer Dave Abbruzzese, Axl has collaborated with more people in a few years than the average musician does in a lifetime.

Axl is adamant he tried all he could to keep Guns afloat in the manner it was accustomed to. But the truth is Slash and Duff stayed as long as they could before eventually realising Guns was never going to be the same again.

"The same kind of thing was going on when Guns N' Roses started out," Slash told *Guitar World* about his renewed spirit for rock. "I'm going with my gut feeling. Everybody is confused right now, but I think people are really hungry for a good hard rock record and we're one of the only hard rock bands who are about to put out a new record. Plus, the reaction has been great when we've played the new songs live. As far as I am concerned, a record shouldn't be recorded until the songs have come together through being played live. Songs develop so much better after you've played them in front of an audience. The songs really kick ass, which is what a hard rock song is supposed to do. But you can't think about these things too much. Rock and roll is best when you recognise it for what it is and you don't try to make it into something that it shouldn't be."

Though the forthcoming Snakepit album was anything but throwaway or predictable – in fact it was quite the opposite – the ever present modesty of the mulatto guitarist was present in every interview he conducted regarding his new band. "The thing is, we did it really quick," he said of the album. "It wasn't necessarily supposed to be taken seriously, because I didn't know what I was doing. It wasn't like I didn't want to play it to anybody; it was just a glorified demo. That's really what it came down to. And as I realised the gap between the end of the last Guns' tour and the beginning of the making of the next Guns' record started to widen, then I started to realise that there were more and more things I could do with it ... at the beginning I did say, 'I don't wanna play this for anybody. I don't know exactly what this is for' ... we didn't even have a name at the time. It was just a bunch of guys."

The album *It's Five O'Clock Somewhere* was issued in March 1995, almost as if by mistake. Slash almost felt as if it were undeserved of a major release, such was his humility. For many years, the ever reliable Axl and his highly quotable persona had led the way in media interviews and headlines. Suddenly Slash was the sole focal point and it felt a little strange. It helped, of course, having Matt Sorum and Gilby Clarke in tow and along for the ride, but in truth there was a good reason Snakepit was preceded by the Slash trademark. At least the pressure was somewhat lifted by the fact Slash was still merely a guitarist, he hadn't copied Dave Grohl of Nirvana in dropping the tools for his main instrument and becoming a singing, guitar playing frontman (which Grohl does for the Foo Fighters extremely well). Yet, from now on, it would be harder for Slash to avoid the limelight. If he wanted to carry on playing rock music, as he most certainly did, then he had to accept the fact his fans were going to follow him wherever he went and the music press would want to talk to him more than ever.

* * *

Slash could not play on a bad album, and *It's Five O' Clock Somewhere* was testament to his solo abilities. It was certainly a band but the focus had to be on both the guitarist and Eric Dover. The two were responsible for most of the material and it only went to prove Slash's talent for finding a very capable vocalist. Considering Dover was essentially a guitarist himself, he did a remarkable job at carrying the Snakepit material. Nowhere was this more apparent than on the opening track 'Neither Can I'. A superb up and down number with a fantastic riff which sounded almost as eerie and powerful acoustically as it did on electric guitar, the song was a crashing heavy blues number. This song would be used to promote the album along with its bubbly successor, the 'Dime Store Rock'. Built around a tumbling drum beat from Matt Sorum, the song benefited from both a wailing Slash lick, perforated with trademark Gilby Clarke guitar moves. Yes, this was the blues but it cruised along with the swagger of hard rock veterans. There was a sprinkling of glam both old and new, a nod to 1970s and 1980s Aerosmith with a huge helping of Snakepit's own distinctive chemistry. Everything one expected from Slash was here but, with the inimitable voice of Eric Dover, the music soared to new and previously unexplored heights.

The toiling blues rock of 'Beggars & Hangers-On' was the closest Snakepit would get to a ballad, all bourbon and Marlboro ramblings. The punk attitude gave the blues a new twist and this emanated from the co-credit Duff McKagan received for the song. He and Slash had at one point been working on the track with a possible view to using it in G N' R. One can imagine Axl's unique vocal fronting the song but Eric

Dover gave it a clever enough slant to make it a Snakepit classic.

Another standout track was 'Monkey Chow' with its eerie riffs. The song, penned solely by Clarke, suited the Snakepit boys perfectly. 'Be The Ball' was, however, the true embodiment of everything 'Slash'. It was the only song the guitarist wrote entirely himself, from lyrics to music. Mixing hard rock with pure heavy metal, the song was a homage to just going with the flow – a perfect motto for Slash; the title was taken from his love of pinball. The song refers to a wild road trip soundtracked by The Rolling Stones.

'I Hate Everybody (But You)' was a cheeky slab of hi-octane blues rock, almost AC/DC-like in its simplicity. The album ends with 'Back And Forth Again', which starts with a Beatles-like acoustic/keyboard passage. It then morphs into a Black Crowes-style chorus, with Dover flexing his vocal chords to rapturous effect. In a way, the album ends how it began, with a soothing, trumped up rock ballad, featuring sumptuous guitars and another rousing chorus. It was clear Snakepit had a lot to offer.

The artwork for the album was typical Slash and the guitarist loved the design. A smoking snake wearing a top hat, what could be better! Overall, the Snakepit album proved to many people just how strong Slash could be even outside of G N' R.

It was perhaps a common inaccuracy to assume Guns N' Roses was all about Axl Rose. Yes, there is no doubt that without Axl's unmistakeable vocals and his compelling presence (however controversial), Guns would never have reached the level they did and he is perhaps the only member who the band could never survive without. But, no one should have ever assumed that Slash was any less of a star. When Slash left Guns N' Roses, it didn't destroy the wobbly infrastructure, but for many keen observers, the heart and soul departed with the guitarist. The power and formidability of Slash's guitar playing and natural image cannot be overstated. It's no surprise people tend to remember the so-called glory days of the band as featuring the 'classic line-up' of Slash, Axl, Duff, Izzy and Steven. In those days there were five characters and this yielded huge public interest. As each personality gradually left the band, so the building blocks were taken away until only a small percentage of that Guns' spirit remained. Slash was as big a factor in Guns' inimitable image and their core sound as anyone else and it simply sucked that the band would never be the same again.

Still, the move way from Guns N' Roses did not happen the instant *It's 5 O' Clock Somewhere* was released. His final departure from the band that had made such an impact was far more protracted. In Slash's mind, the new album would probably only be a break from the monotony of waiting for Axl to 'be ready'. Slash fully expected that after the issue of the new album and a few live shows for fun, Guns would be back firing on all cylinders and ready to record their next proper album. It didn't turn out that way.

When he realised Axl was still considering what to do next, Slash packed the guitar and co-operated with Geffen (who were becoming edgy) who suggested a four-month tour to promote the Snakepit record. Only Eric Dover and Gilby Clarke stayed with Slash for the live shows. Sorum stayed at home, perhaps cautious of upsetting an already angered Axl, whilst Mike Inez had commitments with Alice In Chains. James Lomenzo and Brian Tichy were hired to take their places for the shows.

Slash enjoyed himself taking his own outfit around the world. "You can't imagine how much fun I had on the *It's Five O'Clock Somewhere* tour," he explained to www.snakepit.org. "I felt like when Guns first started. I wasn't trying to recapture a kind of magic, I just played with no holds barred, the way I like it. I met thousands of kids and had a huge kick." The return to the world of Guns N' Roses after these liberating dates was a big shock. "You can imagine how brutal the transition was when I came back to Guns. Very quickly, I thought 'Fuck that, it's annoying. I want to play without torturing myself'. Snakepit opened my eyes. It's my band, but above all it's a *band*, a real one that wants to have fun and go forward. I left Guns out of love. Out of love of music and being on stage."

And so, come 1996, Slash officially departed the ranks of Guns N' Roses, seemingly for good. It was a relief to the man who had spent his whole public life in the shadow of an enigmatic frontman, when all he really wanted to do was play guitar. Revealingly Slash would say of Guns' dwindling appeal, "I don't give a fuck about doing epic videos and so on and so forth, or talking about my ex-wife or ex-girlfriend. It's part of Axl's trip – he sees what he's singing. If you asked me to recite the lyrics to, say, 'Don't Cry', the only things I can think of are "Don't cry" and "Talk to me softly". I don't fuckin' know the words. I don't even know the words to the songs I fuckin' wrote in Snakepit!"

While Axl would doubtless have a different point

of view and insinuate Slash was just not cut out for his brand of detailed, epic rock, you had to admire the honesty and straightforward attitude of the frizzy haired guitar god. It was downright refreshing to hear such specific and liberating views on rock music which, after all, is supposed to be enjoyable, as for so many it provides pure escapism. For Slash, it wasn't about fights with security or fans, about verbal sparring matches with the press or deciding you weren't in the right frame of mind to play a show, it was all about the music ultimately and Slash was perpetually ready to rock. He proved it on the *Five O' Clock Somewhere* Tour. Not only was every show sweetly played and to the point, never progressing much past an hour or so, but every date was fulfilled and Slash and Co. were never late once!

Partly due to this short yet perfectly executed tour, but mainly because the songs were so strong, *It's Five O' Clock Somewhere* achieved multi-platinum success, and garnered complimentary reviews in the press. This, at a time when grunge was the 'in' thing and Guns N' Roses trailed Pearl Jam, Soundgarden and Nirvana in the popularity stakes. Predictably, Axl Rose was none too impressed and effectively he disassociated himself from Slash and all the ex-G N' R members, persevering alone in creating an album which, at the time of writing, would fail to materialise for at least fifteen years.

Chapter 11

SHAMBOLIC LICENSE: THE CHINESE DEMOCRACY DEBACLE

"IN ORDER TO BE A SINGER YOU HAVE TO BE AN ACTOR, AND IN ORDER TO BE AN ACTOR YOU HAVE TO BE A VISIONARY. WHEREAS WITH GUITAR PLAYERS WE REALLY JUST WANNA PLAY; WE JUST WANNA GET THE RECORD DONE SO WE CAN GO OUT AND DO IT LIVE. THERE'S JUST A CONFLICT THERE, AND IT'S NATURAL."
SLASH

It is the most talked about album of the last decade and yet, so far, there has only been one full song revealed! Axl Rose's *Chinese Democracy* has reportedly cost $10 million dollars and, as of early 2007, is again reported to be "coming soon". It has been "coming soon" for the last ten years. In fact, the album has been so long in the making that a ridiculously long cast of characters has either been directly or partly involved with the recording. In the first few years of the mooted LP, Slash, Duff and Izzy were all part of the crew. "Axl and Matt and Duff and I had worked on new material," Slash says. "I hadn't heard Axl sing anything, but he was there while we were fucking around jamming. And we tried out different guitar players ... such as Zakk Wylde ..."

Wylde has often been asked about the situation regarding the *Chinese Democracy* album and he said tellingly, "[At that point] there were never any melodies. There were never any lyrics." What Wylde heard over several months sounded like "Guns on steroids!" An exciting prospect!

Rose hired among others: Dave Abbruzzese (Pearl Jam's former drummer), Dave Navarro and solo guitarist Stevie Salas. There was room for Axl's friend (basketball player and rapper) Shaquille O'Neal, Josh Freese of the Vandals, plus eventual permanent members Tommy Stinson and old Lafayette partner Paul Huge.

Axl would often claim the problem wasn't him but rather others who couldn't quite compete with his own artistic vision. He even claimed, "Slash told me, 'I don't want to work that hard.'" This seems to refer to the fact Slash would be able to walk into the studio and lay down a track almost instantly whether that was a lead part or a full rhythm track. Even on apparently complex and highly rated sections, such as the solo in 'November Rain', Slash would almost nonchalantly find the frets in one or two takes and make it sound as if it took ten years to record.

Later, Slash would be quoted as saying, "I just wish [Axl] would get the fuckin' record out so I could see why he took something so cool and systematically destroyed it. I want to hear where he was headed, and what he was trying to communicate that none of us in the band could relate to."

Of the complex where G N' R worked at night, one observer says, "It's a musical instrument convention. Axl has more knobs and keyboards and strings and wire and wood in there than you could possibly imagine could even be manufactured."

As Dave Abbruzzese recalls, "You could hunt buffalo with his rig. It had a lot of lights, a lot of blinking lights, a lot of things that you stepped on. It sounded like a freight train that was somehow playable." According to Rose, "educating myself" about the technology that's come to define rock in the 1990s has been partly to blame for the delay. "It's like from scratch, learning how to work with something and not wanting it just to be something you did on a computer," he says. "There is the desire definitely to do it, to get over the hump of people trying to keep you in the past."

Part of the reason Slash and Co. departed was because it no longer felt like a band; it was merely a backing group with a singer they never saw. "I work with the band; I don't work with Axl when we record." Slash revealed, "I work with the band and we just jam the stuff live, and Axl goes in and spends … well, last time it was a year in the studio, just adding and adding. I don't necessarily agree with that, but Axl's so talented he can go in and whip it out like that. Everything has to be perfect."

Supposedly the lyrics to *Chinese Democracy* are all over the internet, although there is no way of validating their authenticity or accuracy. Demos of purported tracks were even somehow leaked online and a crude 'bootleg' version of the supposed album can be found, though it is illegal to download these tracks.

Even whilst Slash was still part of the band he couldn't comment definitively on the next Guns N' Roses record. "If you were to have all of us sitting here, our different views on the next Guns record would all be very individual," he would explain. "But from my point of view, I just wanna do a brash hard rock record, with maybe one ballad on it. Ask Axl the same question and you'd get a completely different answer."

"I'd love to be on the road right now doing my fifth album or whatever, but the way things are and the way

Guns N' Roses has always been – which is that it'll be done when it's done – the most important thing is to do a cool record."

Slash had simply wanted to get a Guns' record out as a priority, though as he insinuated, it had to be 100%. The problem was, Slash and Axl had different ideas of what constituted a new album.

Whereas Slash would form a new project just to be doing something, Axl would not deign to make a solo record and this irked his guitarist. "I wanted him to make a solo album," Slash said. "You have to know Axl to understand what I'm getting at. Axl's the kind of guy who over-thinks everything. Sometimes it's fucking classic, and sometimes it's just ... whatever. [Regarding an Axl solo album] I was like, 'Cool! Do your thing. That way you'll get it out of your system, and when you get back we'll just be Guns N' Roses.' I wished he had done it."

In 1999, fans heard the first taste of a new Guns N' Roses with the track 'Oh My God' which appears in the Arnold Schwarzenegger movie *End Of Days*. This was a strange, almost industrial sounding full-on metal track recalling Nine Inch Nails.

"I heard it when I went to see *End Of Days*," Slash explained to *Circus*. "And I don't have any real opinion about it. Here's how I feel: I'm dying to hear anything that Axl will release, these songs which more or less accelerated the split of G N' R. I won't systematically say anything bad or reject something I wasn't a part of. After all, although Axl and I were often in disagreement, sometimes we shared the same points of view. When I heard 'Oh My God', it convinced me that my departure had been a wise decision and that Axl and I were definitely no longer on the same wavelength musically. I really can't wait to hear what he has written since we split up. That's his work; he lives for it and doesn't do anything else."

Guns N' Roses have continued to perform live, although not exactly prolifically. Still, there has been much debate over whether Guns miss the presence of Slash and Co.

As Tommy Stinson (Slash's replacement, who was in an unenviable position) noted, "There's people in the audience who have 'Where's Slash?' banners or 'We Love Slash' or whatever, y' know, all those people, they don't leave and they must not be hating it if they don't leave. People seem to be pretty jazzed by the show that we put on. No matter what we do, there's going to be some people that are just not going to let go of the old band. But the majority of the people I see out there are having a great time; they're losing their minds and dancing and singing along. It doesn't seem to me like they miss the old guys."

But the real shame comes in words Slash spoke just a few months before leaving Guns N' Roses for good. "In all honesty, I think Guns is one of those bands that will just be around forever. It'll always be in some state of turmoil here and there, but because we're so close in a lot of ways – we've gone through so much together, we naturally fucking feel like family. It's just the little bickering shit that goes on over ideas and this and that and the other, and it's something that's an obstacle that I think we've always conquered whenever it come up. So I think we'll be around for ever."

Chapter 12

INTO THE PIT

"IT'S EXACTLY IN THE SAME VEIN THAN IT'S FIVE O'CLOCK SOMEWHERE.
GOOD HARD ROCK RIFFS, THE TYPE OF MUSIC I'VE BEEN LOVING SINCE I WAS
FIFTEEN. OBVIOUSLY, THE MAIN CHANGE COMES FROM THE NEW LINE-UP, FROM
THIS MELTING-POT OF STRONG PERSONALITIES. THIS NEW RECORD WON'T
SURPRISE FANS BUT IS NECESSARILY DIFFERENT FROM THE PREVIOUS ONE,
DUE TO WHAT I'VE JUST SAID. WE SPENT QUITE SOME TIME LEARNING TO KNOW
EACH OTHER. I WOULD BRING IDEAS AND THE OTHER MUSICIANS ADDED
THEIR PERSONAL TOUCH. LIKE IN A REAL BAND."
SLASH

Though Slash had officially been an ex-Guns N' Roses member since 1996, one question seemed to be raised during every interview the guitarist conducted. Would he ever rejoin G N' R? Could it ever even happen? The problem was, of course, it was never Slash's intention to leave the band in the first place. Therefore he was really the wrong person to ask – it was all about Axl Rose. Perhaps if Axl had contacted Slash, the former Guns six stringer may have been persuaded to return. However, Axl retreated even further into his shell and took on the mantle of chief Gunner.

In 1996, Slash said, "I just wish Axl would get this

Guns N' Roses record done so I can see what this turmoil was all about. What was the point? ... I just want him to do what it is that makes him happy, because he seems so frustrated."

His comments were almost confrontational, suggesting Axl was discontented and should perhaps release either the record of the century, or possibly reunite with the original members. Slash's words also suggested Axl must prove everybody wrong with *Chinese Democracy*; it had to be better than anything Slash, Duff or Izzy could have written.

In 2000, Slash said, "If someone comes up to me and asks me if G N' R is going to get back together, I say that if it was the original band and if everybody could straighten their heads out enough to be in the same room to do it, then I would do one show if the situation was right. We've been offered millions of dollars to re-group ... but the chances of that happening are pretty much nil."

Speaking with hindsight about G N' R in *Classic Rock* in 2002, Duff remarked, "I have two daughters, a beautiful wife, and a house. So any kind of reunion would have to be a real relaxed, family type affair, like it was in the beginning. I talk to Izzy all the time, see him around. So does Slash. We're friends. It's not

worth screwing that up. You know, Izzy had to leave
last time to save his life ..." His conclusion of the
whole saga G N' R was, "We went through so much,
I mean, not like war or anything, but a lot. There are
things that I can only talk to them about. Things that
not even my wife, who I sleep with every night,
knows, because she wouldn't understand that stuff. It
was pretty heavy stuff. The *Loaded* album deals with
that. It's a little snapshot of a guy's life. A guy who's
talking about life after seeing some pretty heavy stuff.
I mean, in my 20s they were pretty fucking intense."
[*Loaded* had been a punk rock project Duff assembled,
and for once there was no appearance from Slash!]

Slash referenced his ongoing Snakepit project when
he remarked, "Thinking about how people are gonna
react, or how long [G N' R] can be away and so on,
is really only an afterthought, considering [we're]
getting [Snakepit] together to make what I consider a
good record, and take it from there. If we have to start
all over again, fine, so be it. I have no problems with
that; I'm just doing it now, with another band."
Initially, Snakepit had disbanded after a short tour in
support of *It's Five O' Clock Somewhere*, Slash assuming
he would now get back to Guns. That didn't happen.

Yet not only was Snakepit left behind, so too was

Slash's Guns N' Roses' career. His band mates for Snakepit didn't hang around licking their wounds. Singer Eric Dover formed a new band, Imperial Drag, and Gilby Clarke continued to release high quality solo material.

Slash immediately formed a new band, just to be doing something, in this case playing cover versions. The unit was named Slash's Blues Ball and the set list consisted of Snakepit songs plus more traditional blues rock classics such as 'Hootchie Cootchie Man' (Willie Dixon), 'Stone Free' (Jimi Hendrix) and the perennial cover of Bob Dylan's 'Knockin' On Heaven's Door'. Slash enlisted the help of Johnny Griparic on bass, Alvino Bennet on drums, Bobby Schneck on rhythm guitar, and Dave McClarem on saxophone. Also joining him was a man familiar to many Guns N' Roses fans – harmonica player Teddy Andreadis, who had appeared on Guns' *Use Your Illusion* tour. Teddy became frontman for Slash's new project, performing the harp as well as organ and lead vocal.

The Blues Ball toured on both the East and West coasts of the U.S. including one huge festival where they joined Iggy Pop, Sonic Youth, Stone Roses, and the Prodigy in front of over 200,000 fans. No matter where Slash headed he was always ready to spend time with his fans, signing autographs and generally being on call permanently for his legions of admirers. This regular kindness didn't escape the attention of the rock press and several magazines reported Slash's good-natured behaviour, often noting the guitarist would stand outside in the rain, snow or wind just to spend time with those who had paid money to watch him play. It was a world away from the insular, paranoid Guns N' Roses organisation. There, it was impossible for anyone save for the touring entourage to get anywhere near the band members. Axl always had a secular, hidden, private personality, which he didn't want to be shared. Slash was the polar opposite, perfectly willing to talk to anyone, anytime.

The Blues Ball was a fun but short-lived project with Slash realising it was great to go out and play cover tunes, but not exactly the ultimate in fulfilment. Ideally he wanted to write new songs and then play those live. Before he would do this again, however, he made several guest appearances on a wide variety of albums. Firstly he recorded a track, 'Obsession Confession' with the Spanish singer Marta Sanchez for the soundtrack to the movie *Curdled*.

He also joined long time friend Alice Cooper for a show at Sammy Hagar's Cabo Wabo club in Cabo San

Lucas, Mexico. This performance garnered a CD release, titled *A Fistful Of Alice*, and contained several Slash guitar parts. And in 1997, Slash also contributed to Blackstreet's 'Fix', a reworked rock version featuring Fishbone and rapper Ol' Dirty Bastard.

Performing for friends for the sake of playing was okay but it wasn't good enough for Slash – he needed to write new material and he also enjoyed the security of a full-time band. Fortunately, the Snakepit was about to reappear, in a new guise. Slash would be the only member who traversed the first to second albums though. Yet it wasn't merely a case of 'anyone will do' for the guitarist. He always wanted a steady line-up with musicians who could contribute without letting their egos dirty the waters of creation. The assemblance of the new musicians came relatively easily. Having been part of the Blues Ball, most of the new band fell into place to be a part of Slash's new Snakepit. Everything was connected somehow – there was bassist Johnny Blackout who knew Gilby Clarke and had played with both Gilby and Slash in the past. Following behind him were keyboardist Teddy ZigZag, guitarist Ryan Roxie and drummer Matt Laug. Ryan Roxie was a notable six stringer, having previously plied his trade with Alice Cooper. Come the end of the recording sessions for Slash's Snakepit's second album, Roxie would rejoin Alice on the road, leaving Slash looking for a more permanent guitar player. Roxie's friend Keri Kelli was then taken on. Kelli was already in a side band known as Dad's Porno Mag but had also played with hard rock heroes Ratt and Warrant. Prior to those successful bands he had also made a name for himself with the lesser known, cult favourites Pretty Boy Floyd and Big Bang Babies.

Slash was not completely aware of Kelli's previous bands but he was certainly persuaded he was the right man for the job when he saw the likeable guitarist play. "The first time we met was when Ryan had to take off for a prior commitment and I was like 'What am I going to do in the meantime?'" Slash would recall to *Black Velvet* magazine. "And he introduced me to Keri. We'd never actually played together but he was just a nice guy. He was really enthusiastic and so on."

The same magazine asked Slash whether he and Keri could see parts of themselves in the other player. "That's a good question because it's not really a conscious thing that you're thinking about," he responded. "I guess it *is* a conscious thing but it's not a pre-determined thing that you're looking to discover. You just get up together and it just happens. And if it doesn't happen you sort of know right then and there. The way this band works is, it works off itself. It reconstitutes itself off its own energy. So depending on whoever's where at whatever given time when we're on stage or this, that and the other, we sort of revitalise ourselves being together. I feed off of him, he feeds off of Matt, I feed off of Matt, I'm feeding off of Matt feeding off of him…It's sort of like a football team!"

Keeping it in the family as always, the singer Slash eventually contacted already knew Johnny Blackout and it was this camaraderie which helped young Rod Jackson to get the job. With some humility the singer didn't think he would be hired, given he was apparently up against some more well-known faces. "I went, 'Aw fuck, there's no way that I'm going to get this gig, [but] it turned out that I got it …I think I got to know them. I really got to know everybody well. I think a lot of the singers that got there, just did their thing and left. I wanted to get to know everybody." This was certainly key to being able to play with Slash – a laid-back friendliness not generally exhibited by so called bigger names who often trailed into a rehearsal room behind their Marshall stack-sized ego.

Additionally, Jackson did not come into the room

with a host of 1980s sleaze rock influences. He preferred classic blues and soul crooners like Marvin Gaye, Al Green and Stevie Wonder as well as the essential Steven Tyler and Robert Plant. Jackson was also of the opinion that this was an equal band, not just a Slash project, something Slash himself was in agreement with and appreciated. "When we're playing up there everybody is just pulling their weight and doing their thing," Jackson would say.

The natural step was to write and record a healthy dose of rock 'n' roll together. "Once the band got together and it became a band, we culminated all this material and decided to make a record," Slash would say. "You just keep plodding along, just trying to progress as best as possible from one day to the next. As a glimmer of light starts to come over the curvature of the earth, you start to see where you're going and then you focus on it."

Still, according to Slash, the second Snakepit album should not be counted as such. "It doesn't really count as a second record because the first record was a project," he said cryptically, "it was just a fun thing to do. I never really had any set intention on taking it to where it's at now, since when I did the first Snakepit album, I was still in Guns N' Roses ... when this

Snakepit came around, it's an entirely different band – with the exception of me – but at the same time, I just kept the name the same."

The album would be recorded at Snakepit Studios, which according to Slash "is called that because it's next to a big snake room in my house. When we hooked up, it was basically recorded out of my house, the five of us hanging out in our own environment." And the musical wonders that emerged were a joy to behold. Twelve tracks of low slung, ball wrenching heavy blues – extol the passion of the debut album albeit with mostly different musicians. Weirdly, it sounded just like Slash's Snakepit even though there was a different singer. There was even a new producer. This time the reins were handed to Jack Douglas. Crucially, Douglas had overseen many albums by Aerosmith as well as Cheap Trick and the New York Dolls.

"That's a funny story in itself," Slash said of hiring Douglas. "Jack was the guy way back in 1985 or whenever *Appetite for Destruction* was done when we were looking for a producer. You have to remember, Guns N' Roses was basically the scourge of the neighbourhood. Nobody wanted to work with us. And I thought working with Jack would be a great idea. But the record company, Geffen, thought that collectively that many chemically imbalanced fucking people trying to make a record didn't seem like a good idea.

So earlier this year I'm booking gigs with Snakepit without knowing who is going to actually produce this thing. And I ran into Jack, he showed up to one of our outdoor gigs in Miami. It was one of those really volatile rock gigs, where everything was crazy. Once the show was over and the dust had cleared, he goes, 'I want to do this.' And that was like; you'd have to be out of your mind not to work with Jack. It's like fucking going in reverse on the freeway."

So what of the individual tracks contained within the second Snakepit album, entitled *Ain't Life Grand*? "The Snakepit record's not like what everybody else is doing, I don't know what the fuck everybody else is doing anymore it all sounds like shit to me. But as far as rock 'n' roll music is concerned, [this] kicks ass." He was telling the truth too. The general rock 'n' roll populace were indeed releasing a load of rehashed crap. Time to keep it real and bring in the basics, performed with finesse and precision. With trademark humour, Slash thought up the album title, believing life had brought him a few lumps of shit with his sugar, but regardless he kept a smile on his face and managed to walk through any obstacles placed before him.

The album kicked off with a righteous blast to the testicles in lead single 'Been There Lately'. The track instantly alleviated any doubts whether this new band could cut it. Singer Rod Jackson especially impressed with his gravel-throated delivery which recalled the hard rock frost of The Four Horsemen's Frank Starr, while also referencing the whiskey-soaked tones in the obvious reference point of Lynyrd Skynyrd.

The immediate impression was one of this being a record undoubtedly penned and recorded in the year 2000, but of an LP steeped in homage to its influences and history. Again for Slash, this album was more about stitching hard rocking chords together as opposed to any standout riffs. The type of melody at play during 'Just Like Anything' endorsed this approach to memorable songs rather than mere guitar parts. As ever Slash weaved his way up and down the guitar neck with frenzied precision, and there was no shortage of blistering solos or timeless guitar nuances, but the beauty of these songs was in the cascading choruses.

With reckless abandon, the group marked out their reassuredly old school reverence – there were simply a handful of bands making this kind of music. Most who were still writing this form of rock were long standing bands reluctant to deviate from their renowned formula, the likes of Molly Hatchet underscoring that theory. With *Ain't Life Grand,* Slash's Snakepit was even further away from the caterwauling angst of G N' R than the first album. Fresh from his Blues Ball project, it was no surprise to see gospel harmonies peppering the likes of 'Shine', a lightweight yarn recalling the mystic Eastern-tinged output of The Tea Party.

Regardless of whether this was a surprise for you or not, one had to admire the unashamed passion of Slash for true gritty blues rock. Sure it was not exactly groundbreaking, but since when were good songs not enjoyable just because they were rather familiar?

'Mean Bone' was a slight divergence, given it featured a female 'rap' performed by Raya Beam (a prolific writer, spoken word artist, singer, producer and activist). The lyrics were slightly more glam rock orientated which hummed along to a memorable Slash backing.

The gospel touches returned for 'Back To The Moment'. Though the almost subliminal Slash bends echoed a series of sentimental Guns N' Roses ballads, this sounded more like Joe Cocker than Axl Rose, but it somehow suited the band perfectly. Indeed, it may have made a perfect single, though sadly it was left as an album track only. Where a host of other artists would make the song sound pretentious and contrived, Snakepit nailed it with a hard rock-spawned sense of rhythm – helping the song recall Lynyrd Skynyrd as much as Cocker. Rod Jackson ably demonstrated his voice was adaptable and personable, as he toned down the gruff sound-bites found elsewhere on the record. Put simply, the band had written a wonderful love song which sounded neither whiney nor predictable – simply intelligent, good time music.

But a hard rocker doesn't stay quiet for long and 'Life's Sweet Drug' came treading all over its predecessor with all the grace of a sledgehammer. A straightforward up-and-at-em scorcher, it was short but most certainly sweet. Further switching the pace and taking in a less predictable route came the eerie 'Serial Killer'. With it's haunting Slash backing, the track was carried brilliantly by Jackson, evoking the horror of a killer and the killing itself. This spooky but effervescent style merged 'Neither Can I' type balladry with the AC/DC urge of 'Night Prowler'. But in an unprecedented move which lent the song a further sinister touch, there were young children employed to provide backing vocals. It was a world away from anything Slash had produced before, but as ever the eloquent guitarist turned his hand to a fresh style with typical ease. And the humping drive towards the end of the song gave Slash a chance to truly excel with a solo that recalled all his familiar notes and phrases plus a few new scales to boot. 'Serial Killer' was a true standout on the album.

'The Truth' followed and marked out another trail of rock 'n' roll glory. Seeming fairly standard in its swaggering chug, the chorus truly underlined this as another special track with poignant and thunderous Slash-isms following the pre-chorus. But just when you thought you'd gathered the pace and direction of the song, it veered into a new avenue, surprising and delighting the listener. It was the type of song evident throughout *Ain't Life Grand* – sharing just one thing with its fellow tunes – it was to be increasingly enjoyed the more you listened. As a solo artist, Slash had taken this path, whether deliberately or not. In similarity to not producing lead riffs which stood out (as opposed to 'Sweet Child O' Mine' et al) he and his cohorts wrote music which weaved its tapestry sedately, almost secretly. Before you knew it, you would be humming that 'unrecognisable song'. Go back to the album whilst paying more attention and you could remember all the initial spark whilst also getting to grips with the layered beauty of each and every song.

'Landslide' was one of the more instant compositions to greet the listener. One take of the chorus and no one could forget it. It was up tempo and throbbing but Slash threw in a sumptuous clean guitar break while Jackson again exercised his larynx to show his versatility. With its pulsing hard rock nous, 'Landslide' would stand out as one of the most enjoyable tracks on *Ain't Life Grand*. The title track itself carried an awesome brass band swagger, evoking a true vaudeville charm (it could almost have been sung by Shirley Bassey, 'Big Spender' style). The only thing needed were the dancing girls, although there were already girls providing the backing vocals. Yes it was an almost throwaway glance at jazzed up rock theatre but still worthy of a place on a consistent and impressive record.

Though we were now well and truly in the 21st century, Slash's ideas and methods about rock 'n' roll held true to his traditional musical upbringing. The relatively new innovation in music was the Pro Tools program. Originating in 1989, the first models were crude affairs but Pro Tools would soon develop to become the number one choice for recording amongst professional musicians. It brought the traditional recording format down to earth with an inimitable way of recording and editing direct to a personal computer. Slash laughingly recalled his induction into the digital recording age when he told *Live Daily*, "On a song called 'Speed Parade', I wanted a car sound on it. So where do you go and find a car sound? For me, it's go to the video store, pick out a Clint Eastwood movie and just loop or dub it in there somehow. And they said, 'No, they have these books of nothing but sound effects'. So it took a while to find it, and the way they applied it was using Pro Tools. Once I saw that I would just sit behind the computer, I couldn't stand to look at it. It was just so fucking tedious. That was my first, and pretty much last, introduction to Pro Tools."

The song was strong enough without fancy sound effects, built on a spiralling Slash riff and a hectic Rod Jackson vocal attack. This was the most heavy metal Slash had been for some time, and it's undoubtable this was the kind of music many would most associate with Mr Top Hat. It was certainly a big part of his overall sound and style, though even Snakepit upped the ante with a fast break just over two minutes in.

Here is where the famed car sound effect can be heard – artificial or otherwise it sure sounded good!

Closing track was the curious 'The Alien', a song which had the distinction of being the only track with printed lyrics in the CD insert. It purportedly referenced an alien being coming down to earth, with studied observations on the state of the planet. But beyond this, the lyrics were largely autobiographical. Cleverly written by Slash the words veered between estranged voyeurism and personal skits. Slash even excelled himself with a solo vocal part that provided the song with some personable urgency.

The cover image for the album cannot be ignored. A stunning caricature of all the band members it was, of course, led by a (rather ugly) version of Slash which left the casual observer in no doubt as to who appeared on the album in hand.

Ain't Life Grand was initially recorded for Geffen, but eventually the album would surface on the smaller Koch Records label, after David Geffen left his company and Slash did not enjoy the atmosphere left behind. "People started getting fired and those were most of the people I grew up in this business with, as far as who I was committed to working with."

Concerning the general rock scene, Slash had to

admit there wasn't much to shout about. It seemed the future of music was festering in a mire of manufactured crap – which went for rock music as much as any other form.

"I haven't really had the time or the desire to check them out since I was focused on Snakepit," Slash said of the Los Angeles-based bands still trying to catch a break. "In L.A. there's absolutely nothing exciting going on," he added despondently. "The music industry is going nowhere. It's exactly like in 1985, when Guns was just starting: no good band manages to get a deal and they end up disintegrating by lack of exposure, while record companies release loads of shit!"

Ain't Life Grand was the culmination of a life spent in the music business and because of his awareness, Slash was not about to get fucked by a label or persuaded into plying a style he personally did not favour. This was part of the reason his second Snakepit opus sounded so fucking wonderful. The album was released to a resounding cheer from all who knew of it. Slash was back, and in some style. No one cared about the change in line-up, it all seemed relative, and doubtless the new band could have recorded *It's Five O' Clock Somewhere* quite easily. As mentioned, however, the personnel would again change when Snakepit had to tour. Keri Kelli was deserved of his place in the Snakepit annals and took it upon himself to handle many interviews either with or on behalf of his fellow guitarist. He told *Black Velvet* that Snakepit could offer the world, "a real rock band for starters."

"Actually that's a rarity these days," Slash added. "That's a big statement. If there are any, they probably don't have record deals and can't get one because the industry is so screwed up."

"There are so little new 'real' rock bands, five piece or four piece straight ahead rock bands that are able to get a break these days," Keri continued. "There are a couple of newer bands like American Pearl or Buckcherry, but obviously it's very tough these days. At least we're here and can give it to the kids."

Giving it to the kids included a remarkable opportunity to support the legendary AC/DC in Snakepit's home country. "Opening for AC/DC constitutes the fulfilment of a dream," Slash said with no understatement. During this period, Slash parted ways with various behind-the-scenes colleagues, lawyers, agents and so on, so it was a time of flux.

"Shortly after, our agent gave me the list of bands who had planned to tour in the States this summer, and I was almost petrified when I noticed the name AC/DC. I sent our album to their management and they liked it, so they proposed the opening slot to us. It's amazing! In Snakepit, we all practiced on AC/DC's songs when we were starting to play!"

The hard part of supporting AC/DC was actually playing before such a musical institution and Snakepit were well aware of the reverence afforded one of the world's premier rock bands. As Slash explained, "It's extremely difficult to open for such a band. Because AC/DC's audience is quite exclusive. So we do our thing, without thinking too much, we go straight ahead. Then we join the crowd and watch AC/DC play, the best rock band I've ever seen. That's good, because it forces us to give our best. I hate to talk about the business aspects, but there's no denying that opening for such a big band is the best promotion I could ever have. So many people have the opportunity to hear your music…However, I'll repeat what I've just said, it's above all the fulfilment of my dream as a kid."

One downside was also to be limited in their playing time to just forty minutes, which Slash admitted was "hard. You're just starting to warm up and it's already time to leave the stage! But you gotta play the game, adjust to the situation and do your best during this short period of time. I don't want to hear anybody complaining. It's a job. And we knew from the start that it wouldn't be easy." Humility again.

Also difficult was the incessant travel and inevitable exhaustion from life on the road. Slash had long been the kind of person who was less paranoid about taking care of himself than the average Joe. Many people travelling through a harsh winter would wear extra layers, hats and gloves to keep themselves warm. Or they would take health supplements to keep their immune systems tip top. Slash was quite the opposite though it had never presented him with a problem before!

He wore the same thing whether it was 30 degrees or −10 degrees: leather jacket, t-shirt and jeans. However there was more skin exposed than was safe and though it wasn't the coldest month, Slash caught the flu in March 2001. As it was a particularly virulent case the remainder of the tour dates Snakepit had pencilled in were unfortunately cancelled. Yet when the other dates with AC/DC came about, Slash soldiered on, only to have his flu turn into full blown pneumonia – a nasty affliction spotted at a pertinent time. "It hit me at a bad time," Slash later said in *Steppin' Out*. "I was doing the shows but I just wasn't feeling 100 percent. So a hospital just happened to be next to where we were doing a sound check, so I went in and they said, 'Jesus Christ!' They didn't let me leave. I was pushing myself too hard and I guess what I had was walking pneumonia, and the doctors said to me that I have to slow down. I didn't want to because I was right in the middle of a tour, but the doctors said I had to. It was unfortunate, because this all happened right before we were supposed to go on tour with AC/DC. The timing was just wrong." You cannot deny his application!

At least these days Slash was not in hospital due to a punishing drug problem. "While I was in the hospital I thought, 'It wasn't even a good high'," Slash said, reflecting on his previous heroin use. "So I'm really over it now. It's too much bother and too much of a pain in the ass. It's too non-productive. Especially if you're like somebody like me who has a lot going on. I have too much I want to do. You can't sit in that funky kind of place for too long a period of time and expect anything good to happen your way. You just get tired of it after a while. If it doesn't get tired of you first."

One thing everyone loved about Slash was his down-to-earth manner and straight-talking style. Nowhere was this more amplified than on his short jaunt over to England. "I have no idea how we ended up here," Slash said of his London appearance. "None of the original places that I'm used to playing, when you want to go out and do an intimate club gig, are still here. They're all gone. Every fucking one of them. So I said 'Where's cool to play?' and they said the Underworld." So he did.

Shari from Black Velvet was there: "The audience laughed when Slash proceeded to hump the bollard stage left, smiled when he lit a cigarette and cheered when he took to the microphone to announce "we blew something up!" To everyone here tonight, Slash is God and can do no wrong ... a lethal dose of rock genius he is.

Chapter 13

THE VELVET GLOVE

**"AXL'S WHOLE VISIONARY STYLE, AS FAR AS HIS INPUT IN
GUNS N' ROSES IS COMPLETELY DIFFERENT FROM MINE. I JUST
LIKE TO PLAY GUITAR, WRITE A GOOD RIFF, GO OUT THERE
AND PLAY AS OPPOSED TO PRESENTING AN IMAGE."**
SLASH

The years since Guns N' Roses had been better for Slash than his other ex-cohorts. Though Duff McKagan and Matt Sorum had not been forgotten by the press, and especially their fans, they were certainly of a lower profile than before. In 2002, that was about to change. Ex-Ozzy Osbourne drummer Randy Castillo passed away in March of that year due to cancer, and given Castillo's standing in the music world, there was a benefit gig organised immediately for the family he left behind. Slash was there and so too were Matt and Duff. The three jammed onstage together that night, April 28, along with former Buckcherry members Josh Todd and Keith Nelson. Those with little imagination decided this was a new band which should be called Buck N' Roses. Though the names did not appeal, the ex-Guns triumvirate decided their chemistry was still intact and that perhaps they should get together to create music once again. To celebrate the agreement, the three played a gig the next night at the Key Club in Los Angeles. It was something of a secret but word of mouth made sure the intimate club was packed in anticipation of viewing a band they called Cherry Roses. At 10pm the impromptu group hit the stage launching into well-versed numbers such as 'Paradise City', 'It's So Easy' and a Steven Tyler fronted version of 'Mama Kin'.

"The place fuckin' exploded," Slash said with no understatement. "It was like, 'Wow, this is really heavy'. So the next day Duff and I talked and said, 'You know, we should probably do something with this. So that's when it started, with Keith and Josh."

Of course, despite having currently high profile members such as the ex-Buckcherry duo along for the ride, this was largely about three ex-Guns N' Roses members getting together. It was an obvious talking point for many journalists but the long years which had passed helped Slash to rationalise. "After years and years of doing that, especially after turning into a huge stadium band, your sense of reality, no matter how fuckin' grounded you try to keep, gets a little distorted. So [after they left G N' R] we all had to go through these long periods of growth, and discovery and self-realisation. Really serious downs, [some] chemical abuse situations to get sorted out, and for everybody it was different. For me, I would never have thought of jamming with any of the other guys in Guns N' Roses. I didn't mind jamming with Izzy from time to time, maybe as old boyfriends or girlfriends screw from time to time, but you don't want to go back to a heavy relationship. That's how it was with all the guys. But after all those years it wasn't about the fear of that, or wanting to go out and make a ton of money because of knowing that we could capitalize on that. It was totally innocent and totally naïve."

But anyone assuming this was a pre-meditated move didn't know the guys behind the music very well, as Slash would infer to *Guitarist*, "None of us were hanging out wondering what to do next. I was starting another band, I wasn't thinking about all that. But that vibe that was hard for me to explain, that energy we got from just getting into a room, especially all this time later, was so intense. Then when we got up on stage and played, you know what, it's too awesome a chemistry, too awesome a sound, too unique a fuckin' thing to blow it off ... to this day, we have a lot of people with certain expectations, comparisons they want to make. And we don't fuckin' care. Because the thing that got this going was just a fresh raw desire to do more with this thing that we'd established."

As Slash intimated, despite the band's history, this was not about Guns N' Roses. Nevertheless it didn't stop them asking Izzy Stradlin if he wanted to join them in a group they referred to as 'The Project'.

Izzy, however, politely rejected the offer in favour of his own solo career. Slash also turned to old school friend Dave Kushner, who was no stranger to high profile rock bands having been in the Dave Navarro set up as well as Wasted Youth. He was also a friend of Duff's, having played with him in the bassist's *Loaded* project. "Dave's our secret weapon," Duff later said. "He plays amazing textures and he can handle himself with Slash." It was important for Slash to be able to duet with an able guitarist who didn't have an overblown ego. In hindsight, the band were clearly better with Kushner in the ranks, in this author's opinion.

Music television channel VH1 were invited to record the process of The Project searching for a lead singer. "We heard so many different singers, and every one lent towards a different vibe," Matt Sorum said after they had captured a vocalist. "Unfortunately, the vibes were usually not too good. As soon as we heard the vocals that people were sending in, we knew we were in trouble, and we knew we just couldn't put out some shabby rock tribute. It had to be something special."

A number of lead singers auditioned, including Josh Todd formerly of Buckcherry, Sebastian Bach (ex-Skid Row), Kelly Shaefer of Atheist and Neurotica and Travis Meeks of Days of the New, but all were unsuccessful. It does seem rather intriguing that Todd was rejected given he was clearly able to keep up with the musicians in a live setting. Still, he had a solo career to think of, just like Stradlin. At least Josh Todd had a distinctive voice which was more than can be said for the majority of unknown and unproven people who auditioned.

"Of course, there were Axl copyists," Slash recalled, "complete fuckin' star-struck dreamer types and really, really accomplished singers who just weren't the right person. It's not like we knew definitely what it was we were after, but with our background we'd know it when we heard it. Obviously if you walked in wearing a pair of shorts and Lacoste shirt with a sweater round your neck that wasn't going to be a winner. But we were really open-minded."

So open-minded in fact that The Project almost hired a female singer. Actress Gina Gershon had played with the band for their early live appearances. Other female singers took Gershon's lead and also tried out with The Project. Though Slash and Co. were more than happy to be fronted by a woman, they ultimately believed a deeper male voice would be more suitable. The preference was certainly for a rock-type voice as opposed to heavy metal screamers. This is probably the reason why the likes of Sebastian Bach, even though a very gifted singer, did not make the cut. Slash alluded to having received very positive Judas Priest (Bach's favourite band in fact) style demos, but it wasn't the right mood for The Project.

Eventually, ex-Stone Temple Pilots frontman Scott Weiland offered his services and the band snapped him up. Weiland had been friends with Duff for a while and had recently been socialising with him. He had also played alongside Dave Kushner when he'd performed with the Electric Love Hogs. From their initial rehearsal, Weiland instantly clicked with the band. "It was funny," Slash said, "the day he walked in to rehearsal it was like, 'Wow, there's the guy!' It was like he'd been in the band for twenty years. He had that certain kind of voice, that certain kind of swagger, and a certain kind of talent. He's very creative, and all that shit made him unique to the rest of us."

Born October 27, 1967, in Santa Cruz, California, Weiland had been raised just outside of Cleveland, but moved back to the West Coast at the age of fifteen, where he became a part of the flourishing Orange County punk scene. With his unique voice, Weiland was able to turn his hand to many varied styles of singing, from straight forward punk tunes *a la* Bad Religion to the emotive and more melancholy methods of heroes such as David Bowie and The Beatles.

By 1987, Scott Weiland had formed a band with guitarist Robert DeLeo, Mighty Joe Young. Soon the group renamed their act Stone Temple Pilots. Always treading the line towards grunge, initially with their debut album *Core,* Weiland and Co. struggled to create an individual identity. Despite the success of *Core*'s lead singles 'Sex Type Thing' and 'Plush' the band felt misunderstood. Though Weiland was criticised for his supposedly misogynist lyrics in 'Sex Type Thing', he was actually the opposite, deliberately mimicking a sexist male.

After a tour, the band reconvened to record their second album *Purple.* The result was a huge improvement and though Stone Temple Pilots was still considered an alternative rock or grunge act, Weiland had a greater vehicle for showcasing his adaptable voice, as the album in general encompassed many different styles. It's songs propelled the record to immense success, for which Scott Weiland unfortunately felt the personal ill effects. During the band's most commercially prosperous period, he developed a heroin addiction. In the spring of 1995, he was arrested for possession of heroin and cocaine, and was sentenced to a rehabilitation program. For a significant time, the band was unsure when he would return. Interest gradually waned for the Stone Temple Pilots and its other members became disillusioned. He did return to take the mic for the 1996 opus *Tiny Music...Songs from the Vatican Gift Shop*, which entered the *Billboard* charts at number four. The album was strong but the timing was now out of sync with the popular music of the era, and *Tiny Music...* sadly became a largely forgotten release.

Weiland then relapsed and the band had to cancel a tour they'd scheduled. The remaining members recorded an album without Scott at the helm, the poorly received *Talk Show*, which seemed to signal the end for the Pilots. Weiland however came back to good health fairly quickly and recorded a solo album in 1998, titled *12 Bar Blues*. This was a popular, eclectic set, highlighting his singing talent, which had not once dissipated.

Surprisingly the original Stone Temple Pilots line-up reunited in 1999, recording a superb comeback album titled *No. 4*. However just as the album had been completed Scott Weiland was sentenced to a year in a Los Angeles county jail for violating his probation, related to an earlier conviction for heroin possession. Rather than letting this deter him, Weiland did his time and returned to the band immediately after his release. The band then recorded another album together, called *Shangri La Dee Da*, which was released in summer 2001. Two years later, Stone Temple Pilots would release a greatest hits package titled *Thank You*.

Ironically, given his history of excess, it seemed Scott Weiland was made to play in a band with messrs Slash, Duff and Matt. Part of his musical upbringing had encompassed the riotous Guns N' Roses debut *Appetite For Destruction*. The album made such an impact on Weiland, he lived by it as a bible, both in terms of easy living and how to sing rock 'n' roll at its utmost. He was absolutely perfect for Slash's new band.

So, The Project had a full line-up and it was a damn good one. They just needed a monicker. Slash wanted to name the band Revolver, but Weiland suggested adding Velvet – whether it was a deliberate poke at Guns N' Roses or not, the name was agreed upon. As soon as the public knew a true super-group had formed, the record labels' interest also peaked, and VR was approached to contribute a song to *The Hulk* soundtrack. Thus, in 2003, 'Set Me Free' was recorded. They also made a cover of Pink Floyd's 'Money' for the remake movie, *The Italian Job*.

Come July, the band played its first live show – at the El Rey Theatre in Los Angeles. There was a moment at the gig when Slash affectionately laid his head on Scott Weiland's shoulder and that seemed to drive the point of the evening home: the former Project was officially a real band. Weiland shouted to the crowd, "We are Velvet Revolver, welcome to our first ever show!" The vibrant crowd in Los Angeles included former Nirvana drummer and current Foo Fighters leader Dave Grohl who was spotted head banging during the band's short set. Also in attendance was *Hulk* director Ang Lee who was spotted in the balcony VIP section looking vaguely bemused. There were, of course, some lucky fans also watching from the art deco theatre's laminate floors.

The band kicked off with a fast and chunky cover of the Sex Pistols classic 'Bodies,' which led directly into 'Set Me Free'.

"Doing the gig was worth more than any time in the studio or hanging out," said Weiland. "This was undeniable and the most sonically violent thing I've ever been a part of. Singing 'It's So Easy' with those guys at the El Rey was amazing. 'Sex Type Thing' was sort of inspired by that low vocal of 'It's So Easy'." For his new band mates, Scott Weiland was something of an unknown quantity, both up close and on stage. Remarkably, Slash, for one, had never seen him perform previously. He knew, of course, that Scott's voice would be just right for the material Velvet Revolver was creating, but playing onstage together was the rubber stamp: "The spontaneous chemistry sealed the deal on this whole collaboration," according to the guitarist.

The chemistry was helped by playing a relatively small venue, a policy that VR has continued since. This is in part a conscious choice by the band – they much prefer shows where the audience is not only visible but also audible. Duff alluded to this when he stated, "In the big stadium shows I played with Guns, the lights would be so bright, sometimes we couldn't even see the crowd. I mean we could hear them but that was it. We want to maintain a toe-to-toe relationship with our audience. We're gonna play the small venues."

Despite the fervour with which Velvet Revolver had been welcomed, they immediately faced a problem with Weiland, which had been a potential issue all along.

Though he had been congratulated by a judge for staying clean just a week previously, Scott Weiland was arrested for driving under the influence of drugs. The singer had turned 36 on the day of the arrest, with his crime taking place in Los Angeles at 6:37 a.m. Weiland's BMW allegedly struck a parked van. No injuries were reported. By following the debris and tyre marks, a police officer was able to locate Weiland's car fifteen blocks away. While he was not arrested for the actual accident itself, he was booked for driving under the influence of drugs (allegedly narcotics) and alcohol. The same day Weiland posted $15,000 bail.

Despite Scott Weiland's court appearances for ongoing drug charges, and his rehabilitation commitments, the band managed to record a full length album at the end of the year, which they would name *Contraband*. A fan website which had sprung up immediately after The Project had announced their arrival, suggested the band call their first album, *Uppers And Downers* which most of the group themselves actually liked the sound of. In the end however they decided *Contraband* was far snappier.

"I'm not gonna lie, there were moments of concern there," Slash said of Weiland, speaking to *Guitarist*, "like, 'Is he gonna be okay? Are we gonna be able to take this to the next level?' But he wanted to do it so badly. He was so willing to do what it took to get through this ... it was good timing for him to hook up with us when he did. For the most part there was no support from anybody outside of us. We've all been there and that helped."

"This has been a pretty rough year for me," Weiland admitted. "The whole divorce thing really pulled me through a keyhole emotionally, so I fell backwards on a narcotic slide and had to pay the price. But these guys were there to catch my fall. This has been like a gang. And it helps that they've all been through it themselves a million times, so there's no judgment there. They've all kicked dope so it's not like I'm the lone junkie in the band or I'm the only one who knows what it's like to kick a three gram-a-day heroin habit. Through all the difficulties I've been through, they've all been there. That's more than I could ever ask for, more than

I've ever experienced before." Duff said the band had been through a lot with Scott: "We got him to come up to the mountains, to Washington State, and he was learning martial arts and learning how to live a different way. Whatever happens, he has some tools that he didn't have before."

Weiland also commented on the creativity of song writing and how that process had been such a godsend for Velvet Revolver. "We're looking to get back that same feeling we had when we all first started making music, the sense of doing it for the pure joy of making music ... We were all wondering if we could somehow get it back. As it turns out, the only way we could get it all back was to start it all new. Now we have that opportunity and it's amazing. This music is just vicious, very aggressive and it forces you to lace your boots up and sort of get ready for the fight."

It seemed Slash and Duff were made for Scott Weiland. With the problems the ex-G N' R members had endured in just wanting to make rock 'n' roll, the time was right to join up with a frontman who had been and done everything before, yet wanted a more sober stab at the big time.

"There is no real concept, to me," Slash stated. "We set out to make music we enjoy and can feel proud of playing, music that people we like will want to listen to. As soon as you start thinking beyond that, about wanting to keep up with the Joneses or about fitting in with somebody else's format, that's when you lose the map. So we've just done what we do, and tried to have a cool time doing it." This was an almost laconic assurance in the ideals of Velvet Revolver, namely that there were very few ambitions beyond playing rock music and enjoying doing so. For many fans, this was a welcome theory. It showed how quickly a very strong record could be created when all the musicians were working from the same page.

The band decided to co-produce with Josh Abraham who had previously worked with the likes of Korn and Linkin Park. It seemed strange on paper but Abraham was more than able to produce classic rock music, and he managed to make the band feel relevant to the current music scene, without taking away their own experience and influences. For the rock veterans, they were perfectly aware they could not simply release an 'old' sounding record and get away with it. Hiring Abraham was all about being able to compete in the current music market. As for the label that would release the *Contraband* opus, the band rejected huge pay cheques offered to them by many record companies, in favour of signing for legendary music mogul Clive Davis and RCA. The reason was based on feeling comfortable rather than raking in the dollars. Davis was something of a father figure, having notched up enough years in the business to cover Guns N' Roses career three times over. The deal was modest, but this low-key approach suited the guys in Velvet Revolver perfectly. Incredibly, the public's response to Velvet Revolver's album would prove to be anything but modest – it was, in fact, ecstatic.

For Velvet Revolver to make an impact on the rock world, they needed more than a few live appearances. They had to convince everyone they were not just assembled for a quick fix and that there would be a slew of original material to solidify their existence. The fans were about to be pleasantly surprised by the superb debut record cranked with a slew of rock classics.

'Sucker Train Blues' is the opening number, beginning with a typically noxious Duff bass line (echoes of 'Right Next Door To Hell' from *Use Your Illusion I*). Though it appears first, it was actually the last song written for the album. The introductory guitar licks are played by Dave Kushner and all the rhythm guitars were played on a 1956 Telecaster. Best of all, Slash's solo was done in one take! The band pegged this song as the first single and it's not hard to see why, doused as it is in Weiland melodies much like the most upbeat of Stone Temple Pilots' material. This segues into 'Do It For The Kids', a more seductive and weaving monologue that evokes a certain element of grunge. Though Stone Temple Pilots were often wrongly referred to as a grunge band, their deep muddy riffs certainly belonged in the rain of Seattle. 'Do It For The Kids' was a Velvet Revolver concession to that most ignominious of styles with a dirty eerie Weiland melody. It was not the only song to refrain from the guitar histrionics of Slash's previous work, building on the riff to the track rather than going overboard with any fret wanking effects. This in fact was proof that Velvet Revolver was not merely abusing their individual reputations for a quick sale. *Contraband* brimmed with real songs, improving upon every listen and discreetly sewing its magic.

'Big Machine' was a modern glam rock anthem incorporating such icons as Sweet and T-Rex with a hint of upbeat grunge. The song was initially written by the VR musicians who then passed it to Weiland. According to Duff, "Scott chopped the shit out of it in Pro Tools and gave us this thing that was like – 'Whoa!' Then we played it like he'd rearranged it, and it totally made sense." One of the many songs to recall STP's finer melodies, this has an obvious Scott Weiland stamp. Though the singer wrote the lyrics, as for all the songs, he was echoing his band mates' sentiments with this particular pastiche of high living amongst the musical elite. Drenched with Weiland's trademark sarcasm.

The meanings behind the songs on *Contraband* were as important to Scott Weiland as the music. He had been recently diagnosed as suffering from bipolar disorder and struggled daily with trying to cope with the resulting unpredictable mood swings. There was a battle in his head and his habitual, ultimate goal was to try and maintain inner peace. Weiland acknowledges his mind has clearly been tainted from substance abuse. Kicking his habits oddly exacerbated his unsettled brain and this explains the heartfelt lyrics behind the album. As ever for the singer, each piece is a story related to a real event that he has experienced.

'Illegal I Song' built on a sinister riff and was a short lyrical burst which in truth was rather confusing. Nevertheless, it was a catchy number which recalled long lost Seattle band Gruntruck, especially through the down-tuned axe work. Both 'Illegal I Song' and its follow up, 'Spectacle', were indications of an amalgamation of rock styles which all the band members had either personally experienced or drawn upon in some fashion. *Contraband* was punk, hard rock, grunge, soft rock, AOR, heavy metal, pop, alternative, you could even lay a claim to it being 'emo', in the sense it was evidently moving, touching and emotional. The work was plaintively assembled and belied the so-called dumb rocker status Slash and Duff especially were previously wrongly accused of.

With 'Spectacle', Slash recalled the notes often explored during a *Use Your Illusion* solo and yet he re-invented the wheel, moulding the song into a Velvet Revolver piece. 'Fall To Pieces' came next and built upon a gorgeous clean guitar break with Weiland's captivating vocal phrasing. It was no surprise the song would later be released as single.

Recalling the ballad style material from Stone Temple Pilot's *Purple* album, the song is a strong build up between a quiet verse and a huge chorus. Like many of *Contraband*'s tracks, it merges the various band members' trademark strengths – luscious guitar playing from Slash, Duff's plaintive bass work and Weiland's soulful croon.

The band made a video for the song but ended up having to battle TV bosses who insisted it was too shocking to be broadcast. The video incorporated

Weiland's drug use by featuring heroin injections as well as graphic nudity. Despite the clip appearing as if the singer's life has literally fallen to pieces, it was a nod to the past. When the band were filming they each had their wives present. The song's basis had been Scott's wife Mary and his two children at the point when they were separated; the subject of the lyrics was the premise of his life falling down around him, and therefore to represent the culprit of the scenario, the video needed to show the perils of heavy drug use. As usual, the message was misinterpreted by the powers that be, who claimed it would encourage youngsters to tread down the wrong path.

In keeping with the family vibe of Velvet Revolver, the band wanted to show solidarity for the video's fictional victim of life's perils. Kevin Kerslake was at the helm as the director of the film, which the band shot in Los Angeles, but it seemed all their work was largely in vain with the video myopically being either blocked or heavily edited on most channels.

'Headspace' was also a nod to the past for Scott Weiland, sounding like a cut from the STP debut, *Core*. It was one of *Contraband*'s secret weapons, on the surface throwaway but actually very well-crafted and ultimately memorable and seductive. There were several moments on the VR debut like this, where songs or ideas needed to be revisited in order to procure full enjoyment. And who could argue with such a writhing Slash solo, placed in-between Weiland's almost mournful melodies?

'Superhuman' was a dirty, heaving track absolutely drenched with Seattle references – both lyrical and musical. Another Weiland mystery epic referring to a drug-addled female, the song was really one of the weaker efforts on the record despite being unashamedly heavy. It featured two guitars played simultaneously, both by Slash. Duff also doubled his bass tracks for an extra thick sound. Unlike his usual clear bass lines, Duff used a fuzz pedal for a dirtier sound. As Duff quaintly put it, "It's almost inaudible but it'll rattle your nuts."

There was a 1980s hardcore element to the guitar work on 'Set Me Free', though the vocals were more pop orientated – perhaps one of the only tracks which could have been used for a Slash's Snakepit album. There was the bouncing up and down fret work Slash so enjoyed, and though the chorus was simple – both melodically and backing-wise, it did not detract from the power and enjoyment. There was a loose element to this track in particular, some sections sounded almost like a jam – despite being together enough to hold the track to some sort of cohesion. This was the beauty of Velvet Revolver – they were so punk in their attitude that at times it seemed as if they weren't the best musicians but such was the capability of the players, nothing was further from the truth.

'You Got No Right' swayed proceedings from all-out rock to a more melancholic feel. Here was a Beatles-flavoured acoustic song, which Slash played on a Takamine guitar, recorded via microphone and guitar pick-up, which is very clear when you hear the song. Though it sounds marginally electric, the song itself was the only one from *Contraband* that was written on an acoustic. Slash acknowledged the chord changes were down to him, but Scott put the vocal lines on top of the music [and they were] amazing, and changed the whole outlook of the song. Slash admitted, "I wouldn't have come up with anything like that!"

Though numbered as track eleven 'Slither' was the first song to be released from the album and was an assured indication for Slash fans that this was no passing side project. The lead riff is a full on groove-laden beast. The initial riffs were written by Slash, and Dave Kushner found this way of working easier for him, as he merely added his own touch to the existing guitar lines. It's no wonder the riff sounds so thick, Duff, Slash and

Dave are all playing the same notes together. Weiland says of 'Slither,' "it's a dark, prodding heavy one that definitely has an old STP vibe to it." The solo even sounds like a Dean Deleo [STP] lead. Altogether this was a song which seemed a touch simplistic, but there was something, some spark which captivated the listener and on closer inspection, this was a supremely memorable track, with a blinding Slash riff.

For their third release from the album, the band had something special planned. 'Dirty Little Thing' was set to have an animated video, something that the group's members had wanted to do for a long time, especially Matt Sorum and Slash. The idea was of the band all being aboard a train – the train itself and everything outside of it being animated. The other members could not wait to see each other drawn as cartoon characters; each of them assuming all would suit being made into caricatures. The ideas were relatively easy to bring to life, given every member had its association with a particular item; Slash with a top hat, Duff with his trademark padlock chain and so on.

Motion Theory, a directing team whose résumé includes Papa Roach's 'Getting Away With Murder' and R.E.M's 'Animal', were in charge of directing the video, which was partially inspired by Japanese artist

Rockin' Jellybean, who designed Velvet Revolver's touring backdrop and is known for his cutting edge illustrations of sex goddesses and muscle cars.

Inside the train, the band members were themselves, and would be playing live in the carriage, whilst everyone was partying around them. The idea was for the train to travel around the world serving the dual meaning of touring the world in a rock 'n' roll group, as well as maintaining a hard living lifestyle wherever they went. By using animation, the creators had license to basically do whatever they wanted – with the train going through monuments and city centres whilst being able to change its scale and shape.

'Loving The Alien' closed proceedings – with perhaps a reference to the last track on *Ain't Life Grand*. A terrific building ballad, it was proof – if any were needed – that this group of musicians knew when less was more. The guitar was understated and complimentary rather than obliterating or overdone. Weiland even placed his luscious vocals quietly over the top of the lovelorn epic. It was a bold statement, here was a rock superbeast, who placed the softest moment at the end of the record. They weren't out to destroy the competition – just to sneakily overtake it. Slash found time to throw in another outstanding solo – evoking his most memorable parts on

'November Rain', but this was no Guns N' Roses. It was a band using their own exceptional chemistry to write something truly unique, spellbinding and real. Velvet Revolver deserved every accolade they were to receive from fans and media alike. *Contraband* was a very clever, traditional yet modern rock record, brimming with reasons to be cheerful. You can almost hear Slash smirk as his guitar rings out over the last few seconds of the album. This is a band, a unit, but one man still managed to steal the show.

It was a nice touch that Slash continued to use his fake Les Paul (a 1959 replica made by Chris Derrig in the mid-1980s) for recording purposes. "That was my main Les Paul for the whole record," he would explain. "The thing is, maybe I'm just too single-minded or one dimensional, but as far as an overall rock 'n' roll sound goes, for me when you get it right you don't want to fuck around with it too much. I've only got one other guitar that sounds remotely like it and it's built by the same guy and I got it less than a couple of years ago. He's got an amazing catalogue of guitars, he's built some of the prettiest sunburst '59s you've ever seen."

The guitar playing was so special and unforgettable on the album; yet even Slash would admit that there was less method to his present day guitar work. "In the early Guns N' Roses days, the solos were a little bit more thought out," he would concede in *Guitarist*. "As time goes by, I realise that when solo sections get a little bit complex, it gets to sound a bit corny. So most of these are real improvisations. I think 'Fall To Pieces' had been the same since the first day I wrote it, 'You Got No Right' is now a worked out solo piece but at the time it was spontaneous. I like having more go-for-the-throat solo sections rather than big structured ones. I'm not out to impress anyone, you know."

And there was the ultimate statement. There was not one single note on *Contraband* that did not contribute to the essence of the song – no overblown, indulgent ten minute fret workouts, just good, honest guitar backing. It meant the album was possibly the least stand-out in terms of Slash's guitar parts but, overall, as he contributed so massively to the record it was all for a greater good.

"Making the album forced me to adapt to new ways of making music," Slash would acknowledge. "I'd never written with those guys before, and their writing influences are different from mine. As a result, our writing took all kinds of unexpected twists and turns. Everything was done in the most spontaneous way, and that forced me to adapt quickly from my usual way of doing things. For years before Velvet Revolver, I would just jump onstage and jam with anyone, and that helped me learn to adapt to all kinds of musical situations. I feel that it really paid off with Velvet Revolver. My playing on *Contraband* may not be my most over-the-top, but it's definitely some of my best ever."

After Velvet Revolver shot the live scenes for 'Dirty Little Thing', they headed to Las Vegas for New Year's Eve and New Year's Day performances seeing out 2004 with a blast. For their New Year's Eve show, they played a mixture of their own songs and cover versions, including an adaptation of the Stone Temple Pilot's 'Crackerman'. Tickets were a costly $150. By around 11:45 pm, the band had a quick break before returning for an encore. They then stopped mid-song to see in the New Year with the assembled throng, bringing their wives onto the stage to join them. After hugs and kisses all round the band continued. They finished off a mind-blowing set and would later begin an after-show party at 2a.m. to see in 2005 properly. However, Slash had to cut short his New Year's Eve celebrations when he discovered his treasured pet cat was ill. A family member phoned Slash to tell him his precious feline was ill after suffering a heart attack. The six stringer kept returning to his hotel suite throughout the night to check how his beloved cat was recuperating.

According to fans, the band's second New Year's show was the better, with Velvet Revolver hitting the stage at a relatively early 9:15 pm. They played more than half of the *Contraband* album as well as their third single for the first time live. By the time of the encore, the audience was rapturous and the band launched into two Guns N' Roses classics with 'Used To Love Her' and 'Mr Brownstone', which Weiland again handled perfectly. They closed their set with 'Slither'. In attendance were a number of celebrities including the late model Anna Nicole Smith who also joined the after-show party, by which time the band were heading off somewhere unknown. There were some complaints about too much feedback at the show, but generally the first full year of existence for Velvet Revolver was a resounding success.

By 2005 there were no obstacles facing the band and they were ready to tour with just about anybody. Top of their list was a wish to tour with both young upstarts Jet as well as Queens of the Stone Age, in part to prove they could handle themselves on any bill, younger acts included.

They had already laid waste to England, taking in a

full tour of the mid-sized venues the group had promised to play. The audience size suited the only unmarried member of the band, drummer Matt Sorum. He found the women of England perfect for his nightly conquests, which he admitted, with a glint in his eye!

Later, in an interview with *Kerrang!* magazine, Slash spoke of his time in Guns N' Roses with eloquence and warmth, yet at last put that band to rest as far as he, Duff and Matt were concerned.

For 2005 and beyond, Velvet Revolver is the priority for all concerned and is perhaps the only group in recent times to match the fervour and quality of Guns N' Roses. *Contraband* has managed to exceed all expectations any fans had musically and, in a business sense, the band has eclipsed all record company hopes. Velvet Revolver's long-term ambitions are to make the band an established rock 'n' roll pillar with more albums to create, more shows to play and more people to meet.

There can be no doubt from even one listen to *Contraband* that this was no fleeting project, it was a very real, full-time band of primary importance for each and every member. The fact the group blew up into a huge phenomenon was just desserts for the hard work the members had put into their last decade. The time was right for the five to come together and utilise their experience and know-how. The ultimate and timeless result was *Contraband*.

Contraband was released in June 2004, debuting at #1 on the Billboard album charts, #2 in the Australian charts and #11 on the British album charts. This was an achievement in itself, but to overthrow pop star Usher from the top spot in America was remarkable – an unlikely triumph against an R&B giant who represented the pinnacle of the world's biggest selling genre (Usher's *Confessions* album had previously spent a total of nine weeks at the top of the charts). It was a genuine signal that real rock music was alive and well and still had a strong place in the market. Cleverly, the band were promoted as much by word of mouth as advertising, in keeping with their old school traditions and exactly how Velvet Revolver wanted it. In June alone, *Contraband* sold 256,000 copies in America. The first single taken from *Contraband* was 'Slither' and this also took the charts by storm.

They knew they had written a diverse record, which covered varying styles in themes throughout its twelve tracks. Each could stand alone rather than having enough to justify a few singles with the remainder all filler.

Duff would say, "It's an album. It's twelve songs. It's not a single with eleven fillers. It's a journey." And Slash confirmed, "Every song sounds different. Everything has got a vibe to it. Each song is its own style." And perhaps more importantly, the Velvet Revolver experience was not about trying to recapture a sound used by either Guns N' Roses or Stone Temple Pilots. Other so-called super groups often had an obvious sonic link, to their previous projects whereas with VR, though Weiland's voice was distinctive, the music itself was a separate experience to anything the band members had produced in the past.

Scott Weiland had often suffered for his art and with Velvet Revolver it was no different. The singer even revealed he had put as much effort into the group as he had ever done with anything since the first Stone Temple Pilots record. Prior to writing the lyrics for *Contraband,* he had been through that messy divorce, which had led him back into the murky world of substance abuse once again. Nevertheless, he credited the four other members as making him feel like part of a gang. It was a gang of ex-narcotic addicts who did not judge, period.

Duff made a typical punk-fuelled statement, "Our music is very aggressive. There's always that 'Fuck you' element to it. Really that's all we know how to do. We can't play 'nice' or play 'radio'. Slash, Matt and I were always that way in Guns, and Scott and Dave are very like-minded. To me, this is the first dangerous band that's come around in a while, truly dangerous. People are going to say, 'Oh a super group. These guys have everything.' And I can understand that, but we're not coming at this that way. We really hope to bring some chaos back into the whole world of rock."

Velvet Revolver launched their promotional tour in Nashville on October 18, 2004, but before they hit the road, they gave a sneak peek of their set to some three thousand fans via a surprise show in Hollywood the preceding Wednesday night. Originally, the secret show was scheduled to take place on the roof of the Hustler store in Hollywood. This was to be the fanfare beginning to their tour to follow, but officials were not impressed. The city of West Hollywood declined the permit to allow them to play. Instead, they performed in Amoeba Records' parking lot which was near to Hustler. They played a seven song set which encompassed tracks from their debut album as well as select covers, such as Aerosmith's 'No More, No More'.

Along with Cheap Trick's 'Surrender', which the band also played live, these songs had already been recorded for release as possible B-sides. The band also planned to cover the Ramones 'I Wanna Be Sedated' and Queen's 'Tie Your Mother Down.'

Regarding Velvet Revolver, Matt Sorum stated in *Kerrang!*, "This is probably the best thing I've ever done. Everyone just seems to be more focused and there aren't those same distractions like alcohol, drugs and chicks. We have a certain name to live up to I think and we have to represent that. That's why it took us so long to find a singer. We waited for years to do something together because there was either a lot of apprehension or a lot of nervousness because we never thought we could be as great as the thing we once had."

Slash spoke of the band's concoction with candid and observational eloquence. "I had played on Izzy's solo stuff and on Duff's stuff and Matt and I had jammed together here and there. But we never formally joined up for a group until now because subconsciously we weren't comfortable with the idea of being Guns N' Roses without actually 'being' Guns N' Roses. The Guns 'thing' is bigger than all of us. The reality of it is, I'll forever be known as 'Guns N' Roses' guitarist Slash'. But we just never hooked up until the sad fact of

[Ozzy's drummer] Randy dying brought me and Duff and Matt together and when we did that was a huge, powerful moment."

Chapter 14

GET IN THE COT

**"I'VE GIVEN UP A LOT OF THINGS, BUT I WOULDN'T BE ME
IF I WAS A COMPLETE FUCKING SAINT."**
SLASH

Guns N' Roses were always on the edge and arguably their 'fuck you' attitude stemmed most famously from their notorious frontman. The other members were often by-standers to the controversy. Over the last few years, however, many lawsuits have cropped up involving Slash, which are a frequent feature of modern rock music. This book is not the place to discuss or analyse such complex matters – which have included legal issues between Slash, Duff and Axl – but suffice to say, it has to distract Slash, or indeed any musician, from the core love of making and playing music.

One time, Axl claimed Slash had visited his house and made derogatory comments about members of

Velvet Revolver, something denied vehemently by the guitarist. Of course, Slash could not get away from the incident and soon enough (in May 2006) he was asked about it during an interview Camp Freddy Show on Indie 1031 FM. "I'm not gonna go into the whole long thing," Slash said tactfully, adding he hadn't talked to him for years.

As if to complicate matters further, it was then rumoured that Slash was about to quit Velvet Revolver. Naturally the questions came and it was Duff who had to respond. Again on radio, Duff was asked about the gossip which he responded was all "Bullshit". A year on and Slash remained with Velvet Revolver as they gear up for their second album.

★ ★ ★

Where Axl Rose has made a habit of courting headlines with his love life, which is often in the spotlight, Slash has been somewhat more secretive with his own amorous endeavours. Of course, as a younger, single man, he indulged in vicarious pleasures of the flesh, especially during the heyday of G N' R, but he actually wanted to settle down for a long time. He married Renee Suran in 1992 only to divorce five years later.

There were then various liaisons with a porn star, groupies and other wholesome young ladies.

In the early 2000s, he met Perla Ferrar and for the second time Slash was to be married. On October 15, 2001 he and Perla tied the knot at a quaint private ceremony in Maui, the second largest of the Hawaiian Islands. Slash, ever the rock God, wore leather pants with a black jacket and white shirt, while his bride looked resplendent in a white pleated gown complete with floral bouquet.

Married life was happy and peaceful for the couple until in February 2004. The *New York Post* broke a story that Slash had to break up a "cat fight" between his wife and another guest at Clive Davis' annual pre-Grammy bash at the Beverly Hills Hotel.

The couple issued a statement saying, "When Slash's pregnant wife Perla Hudson [who was five months pregnant at the time] was heading towards the crammed exit ahead of Slash who was saying goodbye to one of several guests, she found herself surrounded by crowds of guests and media people. As Mrs. Hudson was snaking her way through the crowd, she was shoved by an unknown, belligerent woman yelling obscenities at her." Given her condition, this must have been distressing for both her and Slash. "Police were called to the scene, but the offender continued to refuse to identify herself."

Slash and Perla have two sons: London Emilio has been followed by Cash Anthony . When Slash first became a daddy, the sensation changed his outlook on life immeasurably, making him more aware of his own mortality and the lengths to which he needed to go to provide for his new family.

"It's hard to explain," Slash said when asked what being a father is like in an engaging and in-depth article on www.pregnancyandbaby.com. "I look in his eyes, and he's laughing, and I think, 'Wow, he's real!'"

"He's like another man, he is so into this baby," Perla would reveal. "He says, 'Now someone is more important than we are!'" Slash, she says, "is someone very misunderstood. He's soft-spoken, mild-mannered, the kindest person." Slash even sold his snakes for the sake of the baby, a mammoth personal gesture. And he also had to care for his wife for a period of four months whilst she was pregnant.

"I was prepared for anything," he said, and he had to be, for Perla gave birth early by caesarean section. "He's really squeamish usually," Perla laughed, "but he was right there with me." As soon as London popped out, "I heard him say, 'He's perfect, he's totally formed!'"

Slash added, "My first thought was that he was healthy, in one piece. You have a certain paranoia that he's not going to be okay. I cut the cord, I gave him his first bath, and I changed the first diapers."

Slash even took care of his wife and child in the first few days after the birth. "For four days, he was there taking care of me," Perla said. "He slept with us, and took care of the baby at night so I could get some rest. He was great; I couldn't get rid of him!"

★   ★   ★

Though Slash has often admitted he rarely likes to stay in one place for more than a few weeks at a time, he has in recent years managed to spend long periods at his large main home in Beverly Hills, California. He lives with Perla and their two sons. "Being married, there's a certain responsibility there to a little tiny degree of domesticity – I have to look out for the woman, y'know," the guitarist has said of his home set-up. "And that was sorta cool. Most of the chicks that I would hang out with are pretty much a bad influence…"

SLASH

The legendary Hollywood film-maker, Katherine Turman is a former owner of the Hudson house while there are other famous previous occupiers as Slash explains. "It was owned by Cecil B DeMille. And (director) Roman Polanski lived here. In my bedroom, there's a kitchen; it used to be a darkroom, with girls' names on the drawers! There's also a tunnel that goes from this house almost as far as Laurel Canyon, where they used to have speakeasies during Prohibition. Every house had a basement where people kept their bars. I was like, 'This is definitely for me!'"

Slash, long a fan of pinball, owns various customised machines such as those featuring Guns N' Roses, Elton John and Kiss but he is now a proud owner of a very special personalised pinball machine. "It's a really, really cool game, very different. I drew everything, like I always do, on cocktail napkins. The Guns machine, for one, is the first machine ever made with the real record on it. At the time, it was the loudest machine ever made. The Viper machine we just did... it has Snakepit material on it, and now that's the loudest machine ever made. I went to one pinball company and asked, 'Can you do this, this, this and this?' And they went, 'Umm, I don't know.' I went to Data East and they said, 'We can do anything.' I spent a couple of months in meetings back and forth to Chicago, dealing with stuff."

Slash explains his love of pinball and how it came about. "All the pinball companies are in Chicago. My ex-wife, her family lives in the suburbs of Chicago, and I went there to visit for the first time – I never played pinball as a kid – so I was bored. There was nothing to do except drive into the city and get fucked up and never be able to find my way back. But they had a basement – those are real popular in Chicago – and they had pinball machines down there. So I played pinball every night for a week. We came home and I bought The Addams Family machine for Renee. That was the first one. Then one turned into two, two turned into four, four into six, and next thing you know, I was designing one!"

Slash also has a love of animals and his house is like one giant zoo. "I downsized my reptile collection," the guitarist says. "I probably have fifty snakes and a couple of iguanas and three cats. I've got two new additions, but I don't know if they're permanent. They're mommy's kids. I'm not a dog person. Cats and snakes are more like me, very independent; they only need you when they need you and can take care of themselves."

SLASH

"It's just awesome, every day is a new experience," Perla says of parenthood and family life. "Slash has just been amazing with him. Last night, they were just sleeping together," she explains whilst also saying the birth of their first child brought them closer together as a couple. Slash described his fatherhood in a word only he could have dreamt up – and which, perhaps, could equally sum up his remarkable life and career ...

"It's fantastical."

Chapter 15

DID YOU KNOW?

"FOR THE MOST PART, I DON'T BELIEVE IN SELF GRATIFICATION
BY PUTTING UP (GOLD RECORDS AND AWARDS). I GIVE ALL MY
GOLD RECORDS AWAY; I DON'T LIKE TO HAVE THAT STUFF AROUND THE
HOUSE. BUT I HAVETHE ORIGINAL 'APPETITE...' ARTWORK AND THE
POSTERFOR MONSTERS OF ROCK, THE FIRST ONE WE PLAYED,
WITH IRON MAIDEN ON IT."
SLASH

The following is a study of everything from Slash's guitar style and equipment to little known facts about his life and career.

Professional Life

"My Gibson flame top is the guitar I got when Guns first started working in the studio. That's what *Appetite For Destruction*, the whole record, was done with."

Guitars

The centre piece of Slash's career and the one material indulgence he has – the guitar is vital to explaining much about the man behind it. Slash owns over one hundred guitars. Most notably these include:

SLASH

Gibson

A 1958 Les Paul replica which Slash uses on most recordings. This was built by Chris Derrig.

He has several other custom and standard Les Paul guitars including a 1959 standard and 1969 copy. There is also Slash's 2004 signature model used in Velvet Revolver.

Also in the Gibson line, Slash owns a 1960s SG, 1963 & 1965 Melody Makers, a 1959 Flying V and a 1958 Explorer. Additionally, Slash plays the ES-335, Firebird VII and EDS-1275 from his favourite manufacturer.

Fender

Slash also sometimes favours the most popular brand of guitar in the world, the Fender. Naturally he owns the ubiquitous Squier Stratocaster as well as the original Fender Stratocaster models from both 1956 and 1965. He also possesses a 1952 Telecaster and a Jagmaster from 2006.

Others

Slash has everything from the 'posh' 12-string acoustic made by Guild to the more heavy metal BC Rich series. On behalf of that company there are at least three Slash signature models and he also owns a ten-string Bich. More obscurely, Slash owns acoustics from Martin and Ramirez as well as a perfect slide guitar made by Travis Bean. There is also a 2006 Garagemaster made by the company First Act, which was played in a 2006 Volkswagen commercial.

Amplifiers

No guitar is much use without an amplifier and Slash favours Marshall almost exclusively. He was the first guitarist to have a Marshall amp custom made for him and for those who understand the jargon, the back line equipment consists of the following: A 2555SL Signature Head, JCM-800 Head, JCM 900 Head, JCM Silver Jubilee (original 2555 JS, white/silver Marshall head) and a 1960BV 4x12 Cabinet with 70 Watt Celestion "Vintage 30" Speakers.

On the Velvet Revolver debut album, Slash recorded using a small Fender tube amp as well as a Vox AC30 for the more "oddball" sounds. However onstage he uses Marshall amps only.

Effects

Slash recently collaborated with Dunlop on his first

signature pedal: The Slash Wah. It's a hybrid wah/distortion with a red shell.

Other effects used are Dunlop DCR-1SR Cry Baby Rackmount Wah Wah, Rocktron Hush II CX, Yamaha SPX 900 Multieffect, Boss DD-3 Delay, Heil Talkbox, MXR 10-band graphic EQ and the DBX 166 Compressor.

Other

Strings: Ernie Ball Slinky R.P.S gauge 0.11, 0.14, 0.18, 0.28, 0.38, 0.48

Pickups: Seymour Duncan Alnico II Pro

Plectrums: Dunlop Purple Tortex (1.14 mm)

Miscellaneous: Monster cables, Shure Wireless Guitar Kit, CAE custom switcher/router, Peterson Strobe tuner and a Nady 950-gt Wireless Guitar System (used in Guns N' Roses).

Studio Matters

"The selling point of the house was the basement. I thought, 'I can make a studio out of this.'" Slash says, and that is exactly what he did. He claims the studio is probably the only part of the house that is finished! He calls his home "a glorified lounge with a bedroom in it,' and argues – from a wealth of experience – that his studio is one of the finest in L.A. "The drawback is when you come out of the studio at midnight or two in the morning every single night and instead of going to Crazy Girls or McDonald's or whatever and being out, you walk right back to your own fuckin' kitchen. The positive side is that I can be very productive and get a lot of work done. Everything in the studio I've used before. It's that old adage: 'if it ain't broke, don't fix it!'" The entire band can play live in the room which, given Slash's rock roots, is a brilliant facility.

Personal Life

"Slash has called me sometimes about his house, saying 'I've got this refrigerator that's leaking all over the place. And I feel comfortable just leaving it that way, but I know I can't do that 'cos this is my house'." Axl Rose on Slash

An interesting analysis of Slash's handwriting was produced in *Metal Hammer* magazine at the end of the 1990s and the findings state that the guitarist:

Thinking Patterns
The writer tends to take issues at face value,

attempting simplicity in thought, with no 'alternative agenda' in communication with others.

Personal Characteristics

The writer is highly idealistic and artistic. Much of the motivation from which the writer operates is concerned with the satisfaction of completing a job successfully and to a high standard. The material rewards appear to be of a lesser importance, and it is suggested that the writer has an opinion of money which suggests it is strictly a necessary evil. The writer is likely to be generous with money, particularly towards those less fortunate.

The writer appears to have a relatively low 'goal orientated' outlook in terms of money, and considers working at something which is enjoyed to be of considerable benefit.

Having much energy, the writer can be emotionally intense. and it likely to 'pick up' tension from others in a working environment. Under normal circumstance, this is released through physical activity.

Relationships With Others

The script suggests a writer who is friendly and kind to others, and has a degree of vanity. It may suggest that clothes are particularly important to this person.

The writer has a great need of the company of other people, and considers relationships to be important. It is possible that the writer finds much expression in physical activity, but is unlikely to be a keen sportsperson.

Slash On His Heroes (from *NME*, October 7, 2000)

"I like the Pretenders' *James Honeyman-Scott*; the Cars' *Elliot Easton,* who is one of the best lead players of the last twenty five years; *Joe Walsh,* who's one of the best rock and roll guitar players of all-time; and the Sex Pistols' *Steve Jones.* I'm also a fan of Elvis Presley's guitarist *Scotty Moore* and (surf-rock guitarist) *Dick Dale* – to this day I haven't had the balls to sit down and learn one of his songs. And I shouldn't forget

David Lindley, who played with Jackson Browne for years. It might surprise some people to hear me say it, but the dude is incredible."

Al Pacino: "He's one of my all-time favourite actors, just because he's so dedicated to his craft. I guess you'd call him a method actor, although he's done some really cool character stuff. That Warren Beatty movie as the cartoon, *Dick Tracy*. Now I wasn't a Dick Tracy fan, but he was great in that. And yesterday I saw *Scent Of A Woman* and he finally got an Academy Award, so he's definitely a hero I look up to for achieving. I've never met him. I get so star-struck if I meet anybody. I met the little girl from the Diet Pepsi commercials and I was flabbergasted! She's, like, seven!"

Vincent Price: "I grew up with radio tapes, not movies, but radio tapes from when I lived in England. He was a hero of mine right up until he passed away. Right before he died he still managed to do a very dignified role in *Edward Scissorhands*. That's why he's a hero: because he accomplished things all the way until his pulse ran out, and that's what he was dedicated to and he had a lot of passion. I saw him in Michael Jackson's 'Thriller' video, but that doesn't count necessarily. He was always cool regardless."

Steven Tyler: "All the shit that he went through, from serious excesses to the point of almost breaking up, and pulling it back together and still being a successful unit, which to me is impressive. Actually the whole band is impressive."

Ronnie Wood: "I've known him since I was like twelve or thirteen years old. I met him through one of my villains. Ron's a hero because he's been doing it since fucking… before I was born. He's one of the nicest, most sincere, funniest people I know. He's a fucking unbelievable guitar player."

Slash On His Villains

Captain Hook: "I always loved Captain Hook. Not the movie version, the fucking cartoon. I love that character and for what reasons? I have no fucking clue. He got his hand bitten off by a crocodile and he just had the fucking look. He's great, and that's about as in-depth I can get about his character. And he seemed to have a soft side to him too, even though he was dead set on killing Peter Pan. He was also very camp."

Sid Vicious: "Sid Vicious, of course, because you can't have a list of villains without him. He's probably one of the most confused villains of all; he's sort of a hero/villain kinda thing. To any mother at that time, especially in England, he was definitely a fucking villain, even more so than Johnny Rotten …'"

SLASH

Quick Facts And Trivia

* Slash has twelve domestic cats.
* At one stage he also had 180 permanent snakes in his house. He still owns rare snakes, particularly his albino boa constrictors.
* Slash has almost shaved his hair off a few times when in extreme heat but has always survived by just putting it in a pony tail.
* If Slash could be in any other band he would choose 1970s funksters Parliament.
* The first band Slash played in was called Tidus Solan.
* Slash stands at 5' 10.5" tall.
* Slash shares his birthday with Stephanie Seymour (Axl Rose's most high profile lover).
* Slash has a "recurring dream which has been going on since the Guns N' Roses days, where you're walking out in front of an audience and the band completely, irretrievably falls apart on stage."
* The company Knucklebonz have released a Slash action figure complete with bare chest, top hat and cigarette.
* Slash appeared in the cartoon *Kid Notorious* lending his voice to his own character.
* His solo for 'November Rain' ranked #6 in *Guitar*

World magazines 'Top 100 Greatest Guitar Solos Of All Time'.

* Slash was not the only member of G N' R born outside of America – original bass player Ole Beich hails from Denmark.

* In the movie *Six String Samurai* the villain Death is based on Slash, featuring top hat, electric guitar and long curly hair.

* In a Halloween special of the *Homestar Runner* series, the character Homsar is dressed up as Slash.

* The video game *Final Fight* features two characters dressed in leather called Slash and Axl.

* In 1992 Slash was invited to become the official promoter of Black Death vodka which he accepted.
  The special signature bottles came in a black coffin themed box bearing an emblem of a top hat wearing skeleton.

* It is thought that Otto, a heavy metal loving character in *The Simpsons*, was based on Slash. Clues include Otto's love of snakes and long black curly hair.

* In the 100th episode of the cartoon *South Park*, called 'I'm A Little Bit Country' there appears a character playing in an anti-war band who closely

resembles Slash, being as he wears a top hat and has bushy black hair.

* In the role-playing video game *Chrono Trigger* there appears a character called Slash, surely based on the great guitarist.

* Slash briefly appears in the Howard Stern movie *Private Parts*.

* Slash once stated in an *NME* interview that he would like to meet fellow Stoke native Robbie Williams. "He's a pop guy, so I'm not real familiar with him, but I guess we're both from Stoke. It would be interesting to meet him sometime to see if we can compare Stoke-On-Trent stories or some shit," he said.

* Slash has appeared in two television commercials – in 2001 he promoted Visa Mastercard while in 2006 he appeared in an advert for Volkswagen.

DISCOGRAPHY

SINGLES:

With Guns N' Roses

It's So Easy/Mr. Brownstone 7"/12"   *1987*
GEFFEN GEF22
It's So Easy/Mr. Brownstone

Welcome To The Jungle 7"/12"/CD   *1987*
GEFFEN GEF30
Welcome To The Jungle/Whole Lotta Rosie (Live)/
It's So Easy (Live)/Knockin' On Heaven's Door (Live)

Sweet Child O' Mine 7"/12"/CD   *1988*
GEFFEN GEF 43
Sweet Child O' Mine/Out Ta Get Me/Rocket Queen

Paradise City 7"/12"/CD   *1989*
GEFFEN GEF 50
Paradise City /Used To Love Her/Anything Goes

SLASH

Patience 7"/12"/CD   *1989*
GEFFEN GEF 56
Patience/Rocket Queen/W. Axl Rose Interview

Nightrain 7"/12"/CD   *1989*
GEFFEN GEF 60
Nightrain/Reckless Life/Knockin' On Heaven's Door

You Could Be Mine 7"/12"/CD/Cassette   *1991*
GEFFEN GFSC 6
Patience/Civil War

Don't Cry (Original) 7"/12"/CD/Cassette   *1991*
GEFFEN GFSC 9
Don't Cry (Original)/Don't Cry (Alt. Lyrics)/Don't Cry (Demo)

Live And Let Die 7"/12"/CD/Cassette   *1991*
GEFFEN GFSC 17
Live And Let Die/Live And Let Die (Live)

November Rain 7"/12"/CD/Cassette   *1992*
GEFFEN GFST 18
November Rain/Sweet Child O' Mine/Patience

Knockin' On Heaven's Door 7"/12"/CD/Cassette   *1992*
GEFFEN GFS 21
Knockin' On Heaven's Door (LP Version)/
Knockin' On Heaven's Door (Live)

Yesterdays 7"/12"/CD/Cassette   *1992*
GEFFEN GFS 27
Yesterdays/November Rain/Yesterdays (Live)

Civil War 7"/12"/CD   *1993*
GEFFEN GFSTD 43
Civil War/Garden Of Eden/Dead Horse/Interview With Slash

DISCOGRAPHY

Estranged CD *1993*
GEFFEN GED 21868
Estranged/The Garden/Sweet Child O' Mine/November Rain

Ain't It Fun CD *1993*
GEFFEN GED 21871
Ain't It Fun/Down On The Farm/Attitude

Since I Don't Have You 7"/CD *1994*
GEFFEN GFSJB 70
Since I Don't Have You/
You Can't Put Your Arms Around A Memory/Attitude

With Slash's Snakepit

Beggars & Hangers On *1995*
GEFFEN GEFDM 21970
Beggars & Hangers-On/Beggars & Hangers-On (LP Version)/
Dime Store Rock/Good To Be Alive

Good To Be Alive *1995*
GEFFEN GEFDM 22058
Good To Be Alive (LP Version)/Good To Be Alive (Edit)/
Neither Can I (Live)/Back And Forth Again (Live)

Neither Can I *1995*
GEFFEN GEFDM 22058
Neither Can I/Dime Store Rock (Excerpt)/
What Do You Want To Be(Excerpt)/
Soma City Ward(Excerpt)/Lower(Excerpt)/
Interview With Jon Sutherland

With Velvet Revolver

Slither *2004*
RCA B0002H2O32
Slither/Negative Creep/Bodies/Set Me Free/Money

Fall To Pieces *2004*
RCA B0002XB8AG
Fall To Pieces/Surrender

Dirty Little Thing *2004*
BMG 8287666142-2
Dirty Little Thing

ALBUMS:

With Guns N' Roses

Live ?!*@ Like A Suicide *Released 1986*
UZI SUICIDE 001
Tracklisting: Reckless Life/Nice Boys/Move To The City/Mama Kin

Appetite For Destruction *Released 1987*
GEFFEN B000026E3O
Tracklisting: Welcome To The Jungle/It's So Easy/Nightrain/Out Ta Get Me/ Mr. Brownstone/Paradise City/My Michelle/Think About You/ Sweet Child O Mine/You're Crazy/Anything Goes/Rocket Queen

G n' R Lies *Released 1988*
GEFFEN B000007ZBF
Tracklisting: Reckless Life/Nice Boys/Move To The City/Mama Kin/Patience/Used To Love Her/You're Crazy/One In A Million

Use Your Illusion I *Released 1991*
GEFFEN B000000OSE
Tracklisting: Right Next Door To Hell/Dust N Bones/Live And Let Die/ Don't Cry (original)/Perfect Crime/You Ain't The First/Bad Obsession/ Back Off Bitch/Double Talkin Jive/November Rain/The Garden/ Garden Of Eden/Don't Damn Me/Bad Apples/Dead Horse/Coma

Use Your Illusion II *Released 1991*
GEFFEN B000000OSG
Tracklisting: Civil War/14 Years/Yesterdays/Knockin On Heaven's Door/

Get In The Ring/Shotgun Blues/Breakdown/Pretty Tied
Up/Locomotive/So Fine/Estranged/You Could Be Mine/Don't Cry
(alt. Lyrics)/My World

The Spaghetti Incident? *Released 1993*
GEFFEN B000026E4I

Tracklisting: Since I Don't Have You/New Rose/Down On The Farm/
Human Being/Raw Power/Ain't It Fun/Buick Makane/Hair Of The
Dog/Attitude/Black Leather/You Can't Put Your Arms Around A
Memory/I Don't Care About You

Live Era '87-'93 *Released 1999*
GEFFEN B000026E4I

Tracklisting: Disc 1: Nightrain/Mr. Brownstone/It's So Easy/
Welcome To The Jungle/Dust N Bones/My Michelle/You're Crazy/
Used To Love Her/Patience/It's Alright/November Rain
Disc 2: Out Ta Get Me/Pretty Tied Up/Yesterdays/Move To The City/
You Could Be Mine/Rocket Queen/Sweet Child O Mine/
Knockin On Heaven's Door/Don't Cry/Estranged/Paradise City

Greatest Hits *Released 2004*
GEFFEN B0001KAA8Q

Tracklisting: Welcome To The Jungle/Sweet Child O' Mine/Patience/
Paradise City/Knockin' On Heaven's Door/Civil War/You Could Be
Mine/Don't Cry (Original) / November Rain/Live And Let
Die/Yesterdays/Ain't It Fun/Since I Don't Have You/ Sympathy For
The Devil

With Slash's Snakepit

It's 5 O' Clock Somewhere *Released 1995*
GEFFEN GEFD 24730

Tracklisting: Neither Can I/Dime Store Rock/Beggars & Hangers-On/
Good To Be Alive/What Do You Want To Be/ Monkey Chow/
Soma City Ward/Jizz Da Pit/Lower/Take It Away/Doin' Fine/Be The
Ball/I Hate Everybody (But You)/Back And Forth Again

SLASH

Ain't Life Grand   *Released 2000*
KOCH 0118752
Tracklisting: Been There Lately/Just Like Anything/Shine/Mean Bone/
Back To The Moment/Life's Sweet Drug/Serial Killer/The
Truth/Landslide/Ain't Life Grand/Speed Parade/The Alien

With Velvet Revolver

Contraband   *Released 2004*
RCA B0001Z2Q74
Tracklisting: Suckertrain Blues/Do It For The Kids/Big Machine/
Illegal 1/Spectacle/Fall To Pieces/Headspace/Superhuman/Set Me Free/
You Got No Right/Slither/Dirty Little Thing/Loving The Alien

SOUNDTRACK APPEARANCES:

The Decline Of Western Civilzation Part II   *Released 1988*
Track: 'Under My Wheels' (with Alice Cooper)

Coneheads   *Released 1993*
Track: 'Magic Carpet Ride' (with Michael Monroe)

Panther   *Released 1995*
Track: 'The Star Spangled Banner'

Curdled   *Released 1996*
Tracks: 'Obsession Confession' (Instrumental), 'Obsession' (with Marta
Sanchez)

The Waterboy   *Released 1998*
Track: 'Always On The Run' (with Lenny Kravitz)

The Hulk   *Released 2003*
Track: 'Set Me Free' (Velvet Revolver)

DISCOGRAPHY

GUEST APPEARANCES:

Sam Kinison, Have You Seen Me Lately?   *Released 1988*
Track: 'Wild Thing'

Sam Kinison, Leader Of The Banned   *Released 1990*
Track: 'Highway To Hell'

Bob Dylan, Under The Red Sky   *Released 1990*
Track: 'Wiggle Wiggle'

Iggy Pop, Brick By Brick   *Released 1990*
Tracks: 'Home', 'Pussy Power', 'Butt Town', 'My Baby Wants To Rock & Roll'

Alice Cooper, Hey Stoopid   *Released 1991*
Track: 'Hey Stoopid'

Michael Jackson, Dangerous   *Released 1991*
Tracks: 'Black Or White', 'Give In To Me'

Lenny Kravitz, Mama Said   *Released 1991*
Track: 'Mama Said'

Motorhead, March Or Die   *Released 1992*
Tracks: 'Ain't No Nice Guy', 'You Better Run'

Spinal Tap, Break Like The Wind   *Released 1992*
Track: 'Break Like The Wind'

Brian May, Resurrection (Single)   *Released 1993*
Track: 'Tie Your Mother Down (Live)

Duff McKagan, Believe In Me   *Released 1993*
Tracks: 'Believe In Me', 'Just Not There'

Gilby Clarke, Pawnshop Guitars   *Released 1994*
Tracks: 'Cure Me Or Kill Me', 'Tijuana Jail'

SLASH

Carole King, Carole King In Concert *Released 1994*
Tracks: 'Hold Out For Love', 'Locomotion'

Carmine Appice, Carmine Appice's Guitar Zeus *Released 1995*
Track: 'Where You Belong'

Boz Scaggs, The Concert For The Rock N Roll Hall Of Fame *Released 1996*
Track: 'Red House'

Chic, Live In Japan *Released 1996*
Tracks: 'Le Freak', 'Stone Free'

The Outpatience, Anxious Disease *Released 1996*
Track: 'Anxious Disease'

Teddy Andreadis, Innocent Loser *Released 1996*
Tracks: 'Shotgun Shack', 'Innocent Loser'

J, Pyromania *Released 1997*
Track: 'But You Said I'm Useless'

Blackstreet, Fix (Single) *Released 1997*
Track: 'Fix'

Insane Clown Posse, The Great Milenko *Released 1997*
Track: 'Halls Of Illusion'

Various Artists, Tribute To Led Zeppelin *Released 1997*
Track: 'Communication Breakdown'

Marta Sanchez, Azabache *Released 1997*
Track: 'Moja Mi Corazon'

Sammy Hagar, Marching To Mars *Released 1997*
Track: 'Little White Lie'

Ella, El *Released 1998*
Track: 'Bayangan'

DISCOGRAPHY

Graham Bonnet, The Day I Went Mad   *Released 1999*
Track: 'Oh! Darling'

Doro Pesch, Calling The Wild   *Released 2000*
Track: 'Now Or Never'

Cheap Trick, Silver   *Released 2001*
Track: 'You're All Talk'

Rod Stewart, Human   *Released 2001*
Track: 'Human'

Ray Charles, Ray Charles Sings For America   *Released 2002*
Track: 'God Bless America Again'

Paul Rodgers, In Concert: Merchants Of Cool   *Released 2002*
Tracks: 'Wishing Well', 'Crossroads'

Elan, Street Child   *Released 1997*
Track: 'Street Child'

Matt Sorum, Hollywood Zen   *Released 2003*
Track: 'The Blame Game'

Yardbirds, Birdland   *Released 2003*
Track: 'Over, Under, Sideways, Down'

Ray Charles, More Music From Ray   *Released 2005*
Track: 'Baby Let Me Hold Your Hand'

Chris Daughtry, Daughtry   *Released 2006*
Track: 'What I Want'

Sarah Kelly, Where The Past Meets Today   *Released 2006*
Tracks: 'Still Breathing', 'Out Of Reach'

Paulina Rubio, Ananda   *Released 2006*
Track: 'Nada Puede Cambiarme'

SLASH

Derek Sherinian, Blood Of The Snake   *Released 2006*
Track: 'In The Summertime'

INTERVIEWS:

Interview With Slash   *Released 1993*
GEFFEN GED 21825
Boston, MA – 15/3/1993

Slash's Snakepit Interview   *Released 2001*
07/02/2001

WEB:
www.slashonline.com (official site)
www.snakepit.org (fan site)
www.velvetrevolver.com (official site)
www.gunsnroses.com (official site)
www.gnronline.com (official site)

SOURCES

www.snakepit.org
www.blackvelvetmagazine.com
The New York Post
Pregnancy & Baby
Steppin' Out
Ink 19
Guitarist Guitar One
Guitar World
LiveDaily
Circus
Rolling Stone
Hard Force
RIP
Metal Hammer
Kerrang!
Toronto Sun
Hard Rock
NME
MTV